Dina

SURVIVING UNDERCOVER

From the Darkness of the Holocaust
to the Light of the Future

Editing and production: Erez Grinboim and Ayelet Kerem
Interviews with Dina: Ezra Grinboim and Dr. Shilhav Kest

Translated from the Hebrew original: Aya Deutsch
English editing: Joy Pincus
English proofreading: Sharon Bar-Ilan
The translation has been published with the kind support of Future Forwards Inc.

Proofreading of the Hebrew original: Margalit Abas-Jian
Design, layout, preparation of the maps and image processing: Anna Hayat
Terminology, comments, and footnotes were collected and edited by the editors

*   Photograph supplied courtesy of the Museum
        of the Ghetto Fighters/Photograph Archive
**   Photographs supplied courtesy of the Clandestine Immigration
        and Naval Museum
***   Photograph supplied courtesy of the archive
        of the Ra'anana Municipal Museum
****   Photograph supplied courtesy of the archive of Kibbutz Hulata

In order to purchase the book please contact: dinatothefuture@gmail.com

This book is dedicated, with great appreciation, to my family: my parents Yehiel Shlomo and Tonia, my brother Marek, his son Sam, his daughter Feiggi, my sister Hanka and her daughter Tirtza, my life partner Bezalel, my son Nimrod who passed away before his time, my beloved daughter Hana and my son-in-law Erez, my grandson Nimrod, his bride Gali and my great-granddaughter Mey-Or.

Acknowledgments

I wish to thank everyone who has supported me, through moments of happiness and of sorrow, and helped me until this very day. This especially includes my family members in Israel and in Canada; the many friends I have made in my life, from childhood until now; and to Yanek and Stefkova from the Polish underground, who risked their lives and the lives of their families several times to save my life and the lives of my family members, during the course of The Great War.

I also want to thank all those who helped me to publish my life story: Ezra Grinboim, Dr. Shilhav Kest, Erez Grinboim and Ayelet Kerem.

Preface

Dina, my mother, was born between two world wars—a time that constitutes one of the most significant crossroads in human history in general and in the history of the Jewish people in particular.

The story of her life is interwoven with these crossroads. Each of the events in her life could have taken a different turn altogether. Each decision she made, and each intuitive feeling she responded to, which caused her to act one way and not the other, saved her life dozens of times or altered her destiny completely. These cross-roads are connected by some hidden webs that could not possibly be explained in rational or linear ways.

We, Dina's close family members, have been privileged to hear her life stories many times over, and it is evident to us that without her wisdom, internal instinct and magical knowing of what to do and how to act at the right moment, we would not be here today, nor would we be experiencing life in her special presence.

This book, which contains Dina's life story, is based on a recorded interview that Ezra Grinboim had with Dina in the mid-1990s, as well as on a series of conversations that took place between Dina and her literature teacher, Dr. Shilhav Kest, twenty years later. The book also includes stories that Dina has told us, her family, through-out the years.

The last chapter contains reflections written by family members about Dina.

We hope that you, the reader, will experience together with us the profound truths that are hidden behind each of the unique and significant moments that constitute the fascinating and inspiring story of Dina's life.

Hana Grinboim
2016

Table of Contents

Chapter Four: The Family

Chapter Five: The Family Members Tell about Dina

Chapter One
Childhood in Koszyce

The Waterwells[1]

I was born in the town of Koszyce,[2] in the south of Poland, on December 3rd, 1924, to my parents, Tonia and Yehiel Shlomo Minzberg. I was named after my dear grandmother from my mother's side, Beille-Dina, who died from a heart attack at the age of fifty-seven, four months before my birth, while on her way to a wedding in Warsaw. I was the youngest child in the family; when I was born, my older brother, Moshe Elli (Marek), was seven and a half years old and my sister Hanna Pearl (Hanka) was about three years old.

My Father

My father, Yehiel Shlomo Minzberg, was a rabbi and a son of a rabbi. He was born in the year 1888, in the town of Ostrowicz in Poland, the middle son of Shmuel and Gittel Minzberg—Orthodox religious Jews who belonged to the Hassidic community of Gur, which would send its sons to study the Torah in the *Beit Midrash* (place of Torah study) in town.

---

1 Relates to an expression in Hebrew meaning "tracing the source of the matter, its place of origin."

2 For further reading about the Jewish community in Koszyce, please see the appendix entitled: "The Jewish Community in Koszyce."

Unfortunately, I have no information regarding my father's family, save for the fact that he was one of seven children. Shmuel, my grandfather, was a rabbi in Ostrowicz, and Gittel, my grandmother, was a very bright woman who knew how to read lips. It was said that she could decipher any conversation between two people even without hearing them.

My father grew up and became a rabbi. He met my mother, Tonia, a daughter of the Lowenstein family, from the town of Koszyce, and married her at the beginning of the twentieth century. This was his second marriage. His first wife passed away from tuberculosis, after twenty years of marriage, and he was left a widower and the father of a son; Shaya was his name. After he married my mother, they lived together in Koszyce, where he owned and ran a big store that sold dresses and footwear for men and women, while serving at the same time as a rabbi. My mother learned how to run a household and looked after young Shaya, who would come for visits, since most of the time he lived with his grandfather and grandmother, the parents of his late mother.

My father's shop was named after him, and it was located on the main street in the center of Koszyce. My father had chosen a life that combined Torah study and work, in order not to be dependent on the wages he received as rabbi of the local community, and in this manner, he raised us to understand the importance of personal independence.

My father was a scholar and he studied the Torah every day. Later in life, he published a book titled, *Mishbetze Shlomo.*[3] He was a warm-hearted man who created many friendships in various social circles; from playing chess for many years with the priest of Koszyce, to

---

3 The book, *Mishbetze Shlomo—Homiletic Exegesis and New Interpretations of the Pentateuch, Prophets and Hagiography and a Few Articles in the Talmud,* by Yehiel Shlomo Minzberg, was published in 1960 in Tel Aviv.

making many friends with whom he delved into studies of the Torah.

One of my father's brothers was an atheist—something that, as far as I am aware, influenced my father's way of thinking in different ways, turning him to be more liberal in his views, to a surprising extent, when considering how religious and orthodox a person he was. The books that found their way to my father's desk had a wide variety of covers; they went well beyond his Torah and religious books, which indicated an open and curious way of thinking. Thus, we grew up exposed to, and deeply influenced by, his unusual and creative way of thinking.

My Mother

My mother, Tonia Lowenstein of Koszyce, was the fourth daughter in a family of six children: Avraham (Avish), Golda, Miriam, my mother Tonia, Sarah and Moshe. Her mother, Beille-Dina, and her father, Itzhak, resided in this town for many years. We have at home a family tree that one of our family members created nearly one hundred years ago. At that time, one learned about one's family tree mainly from tombstones in cemeteries. There are those who say that this family tree contains proof that the Lowenstein family members are descended from Rashi.[4]

From what little I know about the fate of my mother's family, I know that Avish and Golda and their families, as well as Sarah her husband and one of her two daughters, were murdered during an *aktion*[5] in Lublin, in the year 1942. Sarah's second daughter, Henia,

---

4 Rashi—(1040-1105) acronym for Rabbi Shlomo Itzhaki (Salomon Isaacides), was a medieval French rabbi and authored a comprehensive commentary on the Talmud and a commentary on the Bible. It is said that he was related to King David.

5 *Aktion*—a roundup of Jews from conquered territory for transport to the death camps.

survived by fleeing to Russia together with other refugees. Miriam, my mother's sister, survived the *aktion* in Koszyce.

My mother was an energetic and active woman. She managed my father's store, as well as her own household, and was socially active and popular both in the Jewish community and with her Polish friends. Over the years, she acquired many friends, with whom she would play cards on a regular basis.

My mother was not an Orthodox Jew, like my father, and in her day-to-day life, did not concern herself with observing the *mitzvot* (Jewish commandments), either the easier ones or the stricter ones. She left her hair uncovered, refusing to wear a headscarf. Later on, when my father was offered a respectable position of a rabbi in *Agudat Yisrael*,[6] it came with the stipulation that my mother shave her head and dress as a rabbi's wife. She flatly refused, and my father never held a grudge against her because of it.

In a conversation with Ezra, Dina describes her parents:

> Mother was quite mature when she gave birth to me. There had been a previous daughter who passed away. She gave birth to my brother at the age of 30, and she gave birth to me when she was 38 years old; however, my memories of her are of a woman who was 45 years old. A very dominant figure, she was a merchant who did not have time for us. I spoke little with my mother; she was so busy that she passed all of our education over to the hands of the women she employed, including a nursemaid and another woman who worked at the shop. Her detachment was such that when I fell out of the first floor window and came to her,

---

6 *Agudat Yisrael*—A religious section and political party that was founded in Eastern Europe and continued in Israel.

saying that "the doll had fallen," she replied, "Fine, it fell," not understanding that I was referring to myself.

My father was responsible, in our little town, for the donations box that came from American Jews, and was dedicated to purchasing land for the Polish Jews. He was also authorized to perform wedding ceremonies, but he declined, as my mother would have refused to play her part as a rabbi's wife.

My father was not a Zionist. He was a religious Orthodox Jew from *Agudat Yisrael*. He did not tell us stories about *Eretz Yisrael* (the Land of Israel). He told us Bible stories on Fridays. He spoke about things that were of interest to him. He, as well, did not have much time for us; he was also busy in the shop, and the rest of the time he was writing. He made notes constantly, as if he would never have enough time to get down all the things he wished to write.

Life in Koszyce

In her conversation with Ezra, Dina describes life in Koszyce:

Koszyce was a small town near Krakow. It was a home to around 150 Jewish families, and a similar number of Polish households. We lived very close to one another. There was no space at all between the houses; a rather symbolic fact, as we lived side by side, in the same way, with the Poles. There were no sentiments of anti-Semitism, or antagonism, or any wrongful intent. It was a town of good will, as far as I perceived it, up to a certain age.

●

Childhood at Home

The early years of my childhood were pleasant. Our house on 5 Rynek Street was expansive for that time and had five rooms. The furniture had dark colours, as was customary with Jews in Poland at the time. The big chandelier in the living room was lit first by gas and, years later, by electricity, and the credenza, the cupboard containing decorative objects, stood against a side wall. My father had come into a nice inheritance of Jewish ritual articles, including a Torah scroll and a beautiful *chanukiah.*[7]

Since my mother neither cooked nor baked, she hired a team of women for this purpose. A full-time housekeeper by the name of Fella lived in our house (my parents were strict about calling her our housekeeper and forbade us to call her a "servant"). Fella was a young Jewish woman from the neighboring town, Tarnow, who spoke only Yiddish. My mother brought her over from another town because it was hard to find in Koszyce Jewish women who were willing to work in other people's houses and to cook kosher food. Fella cooked many meals in our house over the years and became part of the family. It was very difficult for us to continue employing her after the Germans entered the town. As a child, I loved her very much. Together with her, my mother employed a Polish nursemaid, to whom I was less attached.

My sister Hanka took upon herself from the very beginning to act as my parent—as if I were her child. She dressed me and coached me in my reading. With my brother, on the other hand, the relationships were different. He was an excellent athlete and used to ride his bicycle sitting backward without coming to any harm. My parents sent him to a Yeshiva in the town of Ostrowicz, for a few years. When he came back wearing sidelocks, my mother would not

---

7 The *chanukiah* (sometimes called a menorah) is the nine-branched candelabrum that is used on Chanukah.

let him enter the house, probably because there were lice in there. She cut his hair, and he never grew back his sidelocks; in fact, he probably enjoyed this haircut very much. He was very interested in girls, and courted them with much vigour. He was a nice looking, friendly boy and had many successes with the other gender. I almost did not have the privilege to see him at home. He always arrived late to family dinners. My mother was angry about it every time, and my father used to say that the one time Marek arrived on time to dinner, war broke out... Later on in life, I understood many things that I could not possibly have known as a young girl whose brother was many years older than she. I learned only later about my brother's seriousness and his endless loyalty to the family. Marek appeared to me in later years as a brilliant man, very humane, who had a great sense of humour and excellent business development skills.

We had in our house a pet dog whose name was Pilek. My brother bought the dog in the market when it was still a puppy, for ninety-five *groszy*. That dog was the love of my life. If I were to rate my loved ones at the time, the dog would unquestionably have come in first. My mother allowed the dog to wander about freely, and it used to run to meet me at school. My brother Marek had a sarcastic sense of humour, and he used to utter various witticisms that made me angry, especially regarding Pilek, and quite often, he would go too far, even drawing spectacles around the eyes of the dog. When Marek was left alone with Pilek, we knew immediately where to look for the dog. He would have been under Marek's bed, hiding from him and barking at him. My brother used to make me angry by saying that a dog of Pilek's breed lives for four and a half years (Pilek was four years old at the time).

From daily life, I recall the laundry days. There was no fixed day for doing laundry; laundry day was decided by the laundryman's arrival in our house. The laundryman used to bring water from the well, using a yoke and buckets, and then boil the water inside big pails that were placed on a fire in the courtyard. He would then put the laundry inside the boiling water that contained soapwort, and then rub them on a big laundry board. At the end of the process, the linen came out pure white. During the summer, the laundryman hung the laundry to dry on the roof of our house. On winter days, he also brought the laundry up to the roof, except that often it became covered after a short while with a thin layer of ice. We would then have to take it down to a wringer that was in the basement, and iron the laundry over and over again till it dried completely. My mother had many laundry items, and it required much work to wash them all. We, the daughters of the family, washed the small laundry items on a daily basis.

I was completely sick and tired of washing laundry and, years later, when I was in a forced labor camp, my friend Irka gave me some tobacco that she had purchased on the black market. Tobacco was hard to find, and you could receive anything in exchange for it. I immediately gave my laundry to another young lady for her to wash, in exchange for the tobacco.

The Sabbath and Holidays

The flavour of the Sabbath in my childhood comes up in my mind, and I can see in front of me the table covered with white linen that was decorated with Damascus embroidery, upon which the Sabbath meal had been placed. We sat down to eat every Shabbat with wine for the *Kiddush* (ceremonial blessing over the wine before the meal) and two *challahs* (braided Sabbath bread); my mother lit the candles, my father read out the Kiddush, and we all sang. First on the table were the fish that had been stuffed by Fella's practiced hands. After the juicy fish, there came to the table, in gold embossed plates and pure silver cutlery, dishes of meat and chicken and a delicious sweet carrot stew. For dessert, we were served a wonderful, cold compote—a dish of stewed fruits.

What I particularly remember of my father is that while on the other days of the week he was shorter than my mother, on Fridays he suddenly straightened up and became much taller. He wore different clothes, and his whole figure changed. He used to march to the synagogue in broad strides, as though a king was walking down the street. The Poles felt it as well, and they would greet him quietly, in order not to disturb him in his walk. This image accompanies me all the time; I am caught by it and wish to retain that picture of what he was like on Fridays. On Fridays he was himself. On the other days, it was not his world. Also on Fridays, he would bring an *oreiach* (a guest) from the synagogue, as it was the custom to host someone who did not have anywhere else to go for the Sabbath, and both my parents would be hospitable towards him.

On Saturdays, my mother used to rest in her room, while my sister and I, together with non-Jewish boys and girls, would go to the river, which was only three kilometers away. My father had to agree to this arrangement that we both demanded, because the Jewish young men in our town lacked a high school education, and so we had little in common with them. In actual fact, my sister and I became integrated with the local community in spite of my parents' disapproval, and especially in spite of my father's disapproval. We did compensate my father, for his informal agreement to our outings, by allowing him to teach us girls, on Saturday mornings, upon his return from prayers, a Bible lesson.

Each Saturday, my father would open a different subject, and deepen into it, together with us, the girls, and I had many questions and numerous uncertainties. I recall that Father spoke, amongst other things, about the story of Joseph and his dreams, and about the fact that during Biblical times there were two social classes. The *intelli-*

gentsia—spoke Hebrew, rather than Aramaic, a fact that differentiated the people in all manners from the other social class—the simple people. I interpreted the issues he raised in a different way, which gave ground to many cultural arguments between us. My sister used to take my side, making us two against one. In the end, Father enjoyed this more than anything else, since he was teaching his daughters to debate at length, just like serious Yeshiva boys.

My brother chose not to participate in these Saturday meetings, seeking instead success with the other gender. He also did not stand next to my father in the synagogue, for he had become secular already in his youth, claiming that God does not love *nudniks* (annoying people)... and this is why my father used to be the last to go to and the first to return from the synagogue.

My parents lived in peace and tranquility with one another, arguing only regarding matters of extreme importance... such as the concepts offered by Spinoza[8] and the Rambam.[9] My mother subscribed to Spinoza's way of thinking and, since each one of them had their own philosophy of life, they used to discuss this loudly and with serious consideration.

Jewish holidays were celebrated in our house with a great deal of respect. I recall them because I had my own way of thinking about them. My parents celebrated the Jewish holidays in a traditional and religious way, but I chose to celebrate them in my own way. It is clear to me today that my parents gave me much freedom and

---

8   Baruch Spinoza—born Benedito de Espinosa, (1632-1677)—was a Dutch philosopher of Jewish/Portuguese origin. By laying the groundwork for the 18th-century Enlightenment and modern biblical criticism, including modern conceptions of the self and the universe, he came to be considered one of the great rationalists of 17th century philosophy.

9   Rabbi Moshe ben Maimon, acronymed Rambam, also known as Moses Maimonides, a preeminent medieval Sephardic Jewish philosopher and astronomer, became one of the most prolific and influential Torah scholars and physicians of the Middle Ages.

the room to act according to my own understanding. There was no strictness regarding the obligation to hold a unified ceremonial approach during the different festivities. Perhaps this was because, as stated before, Abraham, my father's brother, was an atheist.

I was probably born an atheist. I did not believe in fairy tales of any kind. One day, my father asked me if I had eaten something between *fleishik* and *milchik*. I told him that my God was too big to enter my stomach and check what I had eaten. Sentences such as this I said when I was eight years old. I had many arguments with him regarding religion, but he saw that I stood firm in my own decisions, even as a young girl. My mother wanted to put my father's mind at peace, and used to try to bridge the gap between us.

My father was a fast reader, and once, when we held a conversation next to the door of my room, he saw Thomas Mann's book, *Joseph and his Brothers*.[10] He turned to me and said, "What does the *goy* (gentile) know about it?" and took the book in order to read it. As he read so quickly, he finished the book on the same day. He returned the book to me and said with a smile, "The goy…knows!"

.

In a conversation with Ezra, Dina tells about her father:

> Years later, when my father began reading secular literature, I asked him if he was an absolute believer. There was a huge gap between us; I was such a secular person out of choice. He then said that only a fool believes all the way to the very end, because then he would have no questions. This was beautiful. When I think about him now, I believe that from the philosophical standpoint, we could have had a richer

---

10 Thomas Mann, *Joseph and his Brothers*, 1933

dialogue today, because back then, there was little understanding between us.

•

My memories of Yom Kippur mainly include my running repeatedly up and down the synagogue's stairs during the day of fasting, and my bicycle riding, as I chose not to fast.

I recall the commotion in our house during the preparations for Sukkot. We had a permanent Sukkah on the roof of our house, and we had only to open it and put branches on the top. I remember well the dances around the Torah during *Simchat Torah*.[11] Since we had a Torah in our house, we held our own celebration with special cakes baked diligently by Fella—egg cakes that rose up relatively high and looked like hats or *yarmulkes* made out of dough. Guests, brought by my father back home with him from the synagogue, would dance together with the Torah around the house.

During Chanukah, we had many festive dishes on the family table. I especially loved the *latkes*—the potato pancakes. One special item my father had inherited from his parents was a silver *chanukiah* that stood on one leg and was as tall as a child. This magnificent *chanukiah* was taken out each year and used with oil wicks for the eight days of the holiday.

Next, I fondly remember Passover. This was the holiday that always caused me to grumble about the fact that the beautiful cutlery and tableware were stored away, and used only once a year, while we used the simpler tableware during the rest of the year. In an especially festive manner, the Passover tableware was removed from its hiding place—two hidden cupboards in the wall of the corridor next

---

11 Simchat Torah (Yiddish: Simchas Tora, lit., "Rejoicing of the Torah (bible)") is a Jewish holiday that celebrates and marks the conclusion of the annual cycle of public Torah readings, and the beginning of a new cycle.

to the kitchen—and it was forbidden to touch it. I recall the lighting of a bonfire that was used to kosher the buckets in which water was carried into the house. This water was then used to render kosher for Passover all of the various dishware in the house.

Birthdays were not celebrated in the house with splendor and many presents, but were emphasized as landmarks on our road to adulthood.

Often, a parade of our Polish neighbors took place in the town. One time, I remember we laughed at the people walking with flower petals in their hands, throwing the petals along the way, in honour of one of the saints. My father told us that a person who mocks the religious customs of others would be severely punished by God— no matter which god. One has to respect the customs of others. He took us aside and explained to us that we must not even smile while watching the parades passing by, because it shames the parading people and tarnishes our faces in the eyes of God.

Flowers never entered our house, in spite of the fact that our garden was filled with them. Perhaps the reason was connected to these Christian parades.

Childhood Vacations

One of my pleasant childhood memories is my vacation trips to Rabka, Szczawnica and other places. I was sent alone on these trips. Since I was a very slim girl, like many others in those times, my parents were concerned for my health, and sent me on several trips of convalescence, during which it was intended that I would eat well and remain in the open air.

My mother ensured that my suitcase was filled with nice, clean dresses, so that I could look my best on any occasion. These vacations took place in buildings that resembled hotels of that time, and were managed by women who knew their business. The guests were girls of various ages, and we were gathered into groups—each group having its own name—in a sort of a summer camp. We were thirty girls staying in one of these summer camps—I remember the number because on one occasion, we were asked to swap dresses, and my clothes served everyone that morning.

Health food in those times included sour cream, butter, fresh bread, fruit and meat, all of which were placed on our tables on a daily basis. Clearly it was affluent families that chose to send their daughters on such a vacation. After my return home, my mother used to pick me up in her arms, to see if I had gained weight. I loved these trips because of the different company. There were nice girls there. We shared girlish secrets in our groups, and we shared with each other the books we were reading. This is how my vacations looked when I was eight and nine years old.

When I was older, I would walk with my sister to the riverbank, where we would meet other boys and girls, spending the lovely days of vacation together.

My parents, on the other hand, did not go on holidays together. My father traveled, for business and for pleasure, without my mother. As an Orthodox Jew, he chose to lead his life privately, and even had a separate bedroom from my mother. Since hotels used to offer only a single bedroom, they could not travel together on their vacations. My mother would go to Krynica, while he used to travel to Szczawnica.

My parents did not maintain a close relationship with my father's family. The travel to their home in Ostrowicz was expensive at those times, and the journey took two whole days in each direction, in a shaky wagon.

My School Years

I spent my first school years in the town's Polish elementary school. Boys and girls studied there together. I was a curious student. The very act of studying became a welcome challenge. I was curious about anything I did not know, such as how the stars were created and what happens in the sky. I was busy with existential questions already from a young age.

I remember well that in the first year, on the first day of my studies in our mixed school of Jewish and Polish children, we were six or seven Jewish children in a class of thirty pupils. During one of the lessons, the teacher read out the names, and when she got to my surname, which was a typically Jewish one, a boy named Staszek turned to me and said directly, and in a blunt way: "Jewish girl, go to Palestine—you killed Jesus," words he undoubtedly had heard in his parents' house. The year was 1931. The name 'Jesus' was never spoken in our house, and therefore, I did not know whom I had killed. I came back from school and asked my father who Jesus was. My father lost his temper in his attempt to silence the conversation about the Christian messiah, with me saying that I had been told that I had killed the Messiah. My father ended the conversation by exclaiming, "*treife, treife!*"[12]

After graduating from elementary school, and because there was no *gymnasium* (secondary school) in town, those who wished to continue their studies had to travel to Krakow or Tarnow. There the girls would be sent to a *gymnasium*, while the boys joined a yeshiva. However, my mother hired the services of private tutors to teach me and my sister Hanka: an English teacher, because of my mother's wish to travel to America, for the purpose of expanding her business; a mathematics teacher, so that we could do calculations later in our lives; and a history teacher. Hebrew I studied with a teacher

---

12 Treife—food ritually unfit for eating according to the Jewish religious law.

named Shlizik, who had returned to Poland after spending time in *Eretz Yisrael* and was teaching Hebrew in the houses of people who could afford his lessons.

Hanka and I studied every morning a different subject for three to four consecutive hours. I studied these topics willingly and with much joy, because I could ask as many questions as I wanted and receive intelligent answers that developed my thinking.

In addition to her clear way of thinking and her ability to handle sophisticated and wise conversations, my sister had an exceptional drawing talent. She used to copy the photographs that appeared in a Polish magazine, entitled, *Kino* (cinema). Truly, she was the one who had inherited the drawing abilities in our family. She used to ask me to sit next to her, so she could look at the figure of her muse. I admired my sister because of certain qualities she had that I lacked. Her drawing talent was but one example. Everything she chose to deal with, she carried out in a beautiful and perfect way. She read from a very young age and used to tell me about what was in her books. When she was older and went to the movies, she told me their plots, and the stories she told were always better than the films themselves. She had a unique and exceptional talent, accompanied by an advanced intellect and superb storytelling ability.

When I started reading on my own, I felt as though I had emerged out of a prison. A whole world of freedom opened before me. I could go wherever I wanted and faced no boundaries. My sister was a very advanced reader. From the age of twelve, she read modern French literature. She used to ask me about the content of the books I was reading to ascertain that I understood them. She forbade me from reading *The Picture of Dorian Gray*.[13] However, my curiosity led me to choose it and to secretly read it. After I had finished reading the

---

Oscar Wilde, *The Picture of Dorian Gray*, 1891.

book, I spoke to her about its contents, and she came to the conclusion that this adult book had not caused me any harm.

Friendships and the Youth Movement

I am glad to have had the pleasure of making one good friend—Irka Chełmiński. What was so special about our friendship is that I did not have to go into explanations about the matters that occupied my mind. She immediately understood me. Irka used to come to visit us from Kalisz. Her parents were from a well-off family there, and she used to come for vacations to her grandparents' house in Koszyce. Her family had close relations with my parents, and this is how I met her. I have a sharp memory of one time in which we ran together in the fields and were utterly happy. In a surprising way, I knew for a long time that this was a happiness one experienced before a disaster—a temporary bliss—and I shared this thought with Irka. It was between the years 1936 and 1937; I was only twelve years old, but my psychological maturity left no room for questioning my perceptions of the reality that surrounded me. It appears that I was a child who was very mature for my age. During that same period, I was also a member of the Zionist youth movement, Gordonia.[14]

From Dina's conversation with Ezra:

Dina: The three main places in the town were for us—the synagogue, the library and the youth movement. The activity of the youth movements began in the year 1934. The two main movements were Beitar and Gordonia. The library contained

---

14 Gordonia was a Zionist youth movement. The movement's doctrines were based on the beliefs of Aaron David Gordon, i.e., the salvation of *Eretz Yisrael* and the Jewish People through manual labor and the revival of the Hebrew language. In Gordonia, the cadets learned Hebrew and the graduates organized themselves into training groups pending *aliyah* (immigration) to *Eretz Yisrael*.

books in Yiddish and Hebrew that served 150 Jewish families. The Jews of the town were not very observant. Most of
the young people were not Orthodox; some were members
of a youth movement, and some were communists, because,
at the time, they thought that perhaps this would save the
world.

A young man came from a different town and established
the Gordonia youth movement in our town. I do not know
if all the children who went there knew exactly what it was.
It was quite an experience, because we had to kind of sneak
out of the house early in the morning on Saturdays and get
to a small village on a hill, where he would gather us all
together and teach us all sorts of things, such as how to fight
with sticks, and to sing certain Hebrew songs, the words
and meaning of which I only understood many years later.

The songs lay the foundation for the future, so that when
we would later arrive in the Land of Israel, it would not be
foreign to us; because through the songs, we came to know
the landscape. He also began, at one point, to bring along
photographs. There was no cinema then, and no overhead
projector. He had been in Israel, and he carried its spirit
with him. He contained that boundless energy of a child.
He knew how to play with us and how to tell us things that
interested us, and this, at home, for our father, was perhaps
more non-kosher than traveling on a boat to the other side of
the Wisla River. We never mentioned it. We had our outfits
and ties. We used to hide them. Mother knew, and hardly
cared, but for father, this meant conversion and departure
from Judaism. My brother spoke a lot about Israel, as well.
Every time he had a fight with my parents, he used to say
that he would pack his bags and move to Israel. This was the
threat he used. But he never fulfilled it.

Ezra: The other Jews, the ones who did not belong to *Agudat Yisrael*; do you recall anything about the Communist Jews? There also used to be The Bund.[15] If there was a Communist Jew in town, what did he believe in? What kind of flag did he raise?

Dina: We had a worker in the shop who suddenly came up with all sorts of ideas. Inequality, she once said, a higher pay and paid vacations—all sort of words that, as a child, I couldn't possibly understand, but I saw that my parents were disturbed by them. They then told me that she had a friend, who was a Communist, and that he was organizing Communist youth, and that first and foremost they were against the exploitation of the working class. I don't know what they might have accomplished, because in any event, the war very quickly did away with them. I remember that this arising happened in 1936-1937. Don't forget, this was a small town. And really, if we speak about 150 Jewish families who were divided into Beitar, Gordonia, the communists and *Agudat Yisrael*, then there was not much room.

---

15 The General Jewish Labour Bund in Lithuania, Poland and Russia, generally called The Bund or the Jewish Labour Bund, was a secular Jewish socialist party in the Russian Empire, active between 1897 and 1920. Remnants of the party continued to exist abroad.

The Signs of the Coming War

Dina: In actual fact, my parents sat and waited. Mother wanted to go to America; she knew that Father might not want to go to Israel. They felt that a deluge was coming.

Ezra: You mean they felt it? Spoke about it?

Dina: They felt it and spoke about the rising of anti-Semitism. I was a child, but I listened to the conversations. Since 1933, with Hitler's rise to power, the inclination was to leave Poland, as it offered no future. We could not enroll in universities. Take the youth as an example; a young woman like my sister, who was three and a half years older than I, after the war began, she could not study in any proper school. She studied with private tutors at home. What could her future have been? Perhaps a matchmaker would have come and matched her with someone she would not be so in love with. So the inclination was to look beyond Poland.

I recall one scene in 1938, as if out of the movies, in which hooligans with sticks positioned themselves next to the shops and did not permit the Poles to buy in Jewish stores. The town's weekly marketplace occurred on Tuesdays, and this was the deciding day. Because we did not purchase with cash most of the time; we paid with promissory notes for the merchandise, and then later had to pay for it. Father and Mother did not always discuss the dates written on the notes, and so it happened at times that they signed notes that were both due on the same date. Hooligans were standing by the market, and did not permit non-Jews to enter. So there was not even a *początek*[16]. And mother stood, inside the shop, with all of her energy; she had been born

---

16 *Początek* means 'a beginning' in Polish—the initial sale of the day.

in this town, and most likely her parents had been born there too. She was like a lady of the estate, and the fact of such hooligans coming to tell her what to do infuriated her. She came out to meet them, holding a wooden yardstick, in a manner very much like a duel, and after a while, she succeeded in driving them out. I saw her as she was, tall and dark, standing there in a duel with the hooligans, and I knew that this could not go on for long. That evening she said, "I am going to America. We will liquidize our business here, and I am going to America." And they registered to travel there. It was probably not so easy; they needed a visa and all sorts of things. But the intention was to leave Poland. She did not want to be there.

My sister Hanka was amongst the very few Jews who had read *Mein Kampf*[17]—she claimed that she had to know what Hitler's plans were. Unlike most people, she believed that he sincerely meant what he wrote, and did not try to repress what other people did not wish to hear. She advised my father and my brother to leave the house even before the German invasion of Poland, and, indeed, they decided to do it.

---

17 *Mein Kampf*—In German, "My War" or "My Struggle" is a book Adolf Hitler wrote while he was at the Landsberg Prison. The first volume was published on July 18, 1925, and the second volume in 1926.

My mother, Tonia Minzberg
(nee Lowenstein), in her youth

My father, Yehiel Shlomo Minzberg (in the middle),
together with his study partners

My grandmother, Beille-Dina

My grandfather, Itzhak Lowenstein

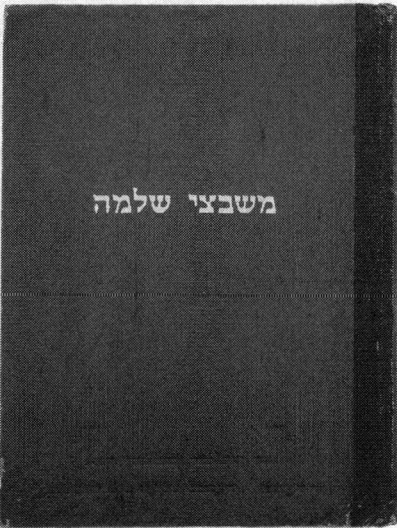

Mishbetze Shlomo,
my father's book

My mother's grandfather, Yossef
Lowenstein—The Rabbi of Serock

Koszyce, my birth town

With my father, Yehiel Shlomo, my mother, Tonia,
my brother, Marek and my sister, Hanka

Hanka, my sister

In Koszyce, before the war

Marek, my brother (on the right), together with friends

My mother, Tonia, and
my sister, Hanka

By the piano, at my parents' house
in Koszyce

With Hanka and young Danushka

My school friends

With Bishe and Irka, my friends

By the Wisla River

Surrounding area of the town of Koszyce

Chapter Two
The War Years

The Outbreak of the War

My family spent the first days of the war making crucial decisions. In August 1939, Father, before his departure, created a hidden partition in the cellar. Behind it, in between the upper wood logs and the lower ones, it was possible to put merchandise. He created the hideout with his own talented hands. He maintained that if we stayed in our house, we would be able to proceed with our lives. My father stashed into the hideout rolls of fabric of every sort and type, taken from their shop to be used later on. Every person needs something to wear, and for years my parents operated a high quality sewing workshop in their store. The thought that, even during a time of war, women would desire a dress that would keep their spirits up, was my father's wise thinking. And so it was. For a long time, we—my mother, my sister and I—made a living from the hidden merchandise that was stored in this hideout.

Upon the invasion of Poland by the Germans on September 1, 1939, my father and my brother left the house immediately. They traveled west, leaving my mother, my sister and me in the house in Koszyce. The rumour in the town was that the fate of the women would be better than that of the men when the German soldiers arrived. And so, the three of us remained at home. I was fourteen years old at the time, and my sister was around seventeen years old.

From Dina's conversation with Ezra:

Dina: The war broke out on September 1, 1939, and my father and brother fled our home. The men fled from the Germans, thinking that this would be a passing thing; that the war would end when it would end; perhaps the Poles would win, perhaps the Germans; but regardless, the men should not stay in their homes.

Ezra: You thought that this would be another one of those wars in which you run away and then return.

Dina: Yes. Because they were certain that the women would not be killed. And it was better that the men would not stay at home, especially men with beards, as they already knew what was going on in Germany. So all the men of the family fled and left the women. What I recall from the war itself is that it began on the Jewish New Year, and the Germans arrived on Yom Kippur (ten days later). They came and asked us to fill buckets of water, and then had someone stand next to each bucket to taste the water and ensure it was not poisoned. As a child, I stood and watched this powerful might, mesmerized by it. I couldn't tear myself away to go back in the house; my eyes were glued to them day and night, as they walked like a lubricated machine. There was magnificence in this strength; I did not grasp the calamity, but only the power and even the beauty. They were so organized and so homogenous, you could tell that not even one screw was missing in the whole of this war machine. On the other hand, the Poles, when on the second day a soldier came with a rifle that was missing its strap and had a rope replacing it, my mother said, "The Poles have lost the war. Because if on the second day he is already missing a strap for his rifle and only has a rope, then this is a clear sign that all is lost."

A German was nominated and placed in charge of the town. There were no SS[18] members in the town. They were *Wehrmacht*.[19] They were regular soldiers, because it was not worthwhile to send the SS for such a small town. Slowly, slowly, different rules came into effect. After a while, they placed a commissar, who was a *Volksdeutsche*[20] brought in especially for this, in the shop and in the apartment. He sat in the shop and sold the merchandise, and we received very little money for this. In today's terms, it would be about $77. We had four rooms. On behalf of the *Judenrat*,[21] they ruled that each family would occupy one room, since there were many refugees from Krakow and other towns who did not want to return to Krakow because soon a ghetto was going to be there. So they stayed in our town, and each family had to contribute.

---

18 The SS—short for the German word *schutzstaffel* (protection squadron) —was the recognized name for the Nazi party's organization for policing and providing domestic and foreign intelligence.

19 *Wehrmacht* (defense force) —the official name of the regular army in Nazi Germany during the years 1935-1945.

20 *Volksdeutsche* is a term that was used by the Nazis to describe "Germans in terms of people or race," regardless of citizenship. The term usually denoted Germans who lived outside of the borders of Germany that were defined in the treaty of Versaille at the end of The First World War. The origin of the term comes from the German word *volk*, which means people, and also from the word *völkisch*, which means "belonging to a certain ethnic origin." The term *volksdeutsche* was a central concept in the Nazi's claim that a person is not entitled to rights according to the concepts of human rights or the concept of citizenship, but rather according to his ethnic, racial and national origin.

21 Judenrat (plural: Judenräte; German for "Jewish council") was a widely used administrative agency imposed by Nazi Germany during World War II, predominantly within the ghettos in Nazi-occupied Europe, and the Jewish ghettos in German-occupied Poland. The Nazi German administration required Jews to form a Judenrat in every community across the occupied territories. The Judenrat constituted a form of self-enforcing intermediary, used by the Nazi administration to control larger Jewish communities in occupied areas.

We gave two rooms to Jewish refugees. My sister, my mother and I stayed in one room, and the commissar took one room. All of this was happening when it was still possible to go on with some sort of routine—to get up, get dressed and live one's life.

By 1942, only a few Jews were left in the vicinity of Koszyce. We survived because the German responsible for the town received from my mother, at the beginning of each month, protection money for the Jews of the town. My mother played an active part in the Jewish community. Her brother was the head of the local *Judenrat*, and per his request, she served as a mediator with the German commissar. My uncle thought that a woman could fulfill this function in a gentler way. She was also responsible for the community kitchen, and when Jews who escaped Krakow arrived after the ghetto there was closed, they ate in this kitchen. Altogether we gave refuge in our home to eleven Jewish refugees from all over Poland. People who were the best of Krakow's Jewish intelligence arrived at our house, and so we enjoyed the company of great teachers who came from the big city.

Ezra: And the Jews who arrived as refugees already told of what was going on, or they too did not know?

Dina: They did not know. They moved on the roads. My mother was a very dominant and strong woman, and she said she would do anything to save the Jews.

Ezra: They were already speaking then about saving Jews?

Dina: Yes. About saving Jews from the camps.

Ezra: Which camps?

Dina: Forced labor camps. I had two friends; one of them was Irka, who survived the war and immigrated to Israel. The second one was Bishe, who was killed in the beginning of the war. We were three girlfriends; we used to go out for walks in the afternoons. We had our own laughter; I would call it the laughter of recognizing that we were alive. We would walk and laugh. My mother once asked, "Why do they laugh, those idiots? Do they not have any idea about the situation?" My sister Hanka was very bright and she said, "Let them laugh the laugh of life. It could be their last laughter." There were people like my sister who read a lot and heard and did not delude themselves; they knew what was about to happen.

Ezra: How did she perceive it? How did she know?

Dina: She read it differently; she heard it differently. When news reached us, people did not want to listen to it; did not interpret it correctly. She said, "I do not believe we will ever return here." In fact, what she did was—she sold what we had in the house and replaced it with things we could take with us, such as dollars and gold coins. She started to give things away to the Poles; things she hoped they would give back to us after we returned.

Ezra: What year was it?

Dina: 1942.

Ezra: In 1942, in the same country, where not too far away so many things were taking place. And you note that your sister understood things that others did not, or that they repressed.

Dina: Repressed. Because in our house, stayed one young man, a German Jew who had been born in Poland. He was one-year-old when his parents moved to Hamburg in Germany. He graduated from Oxford University and had returned to become a lecturer at the University of Hamburg. When the Germans, in 1938, started to send all the Jews who were born in Poland back to Poland, he was amongst them. He came and was really a foreign element. He did not know what they wanted of him; he did not like Polish people; he did not speak Polish at all ... and suddenly he found himself in a foreign country with no preparation of any kind. He married in the meantime a somewhat older girl, a very nice young woman from Krakow, and they lived together. They both stayed with us. He taught us English. This was the beginning of my English. After all, my mother wanted all the time to go to America, so she aimed for us to know English first. So he taught us the English language, and he was also the head of the Jewish police of the town. One time, we sat together, and he said, "I know the Germans, and I know what they are doing. I know how meticulously they do everything. They don't take people to forced labor camps because they can't use the Jews. What they will do is, they will send some to work, and the rest, they will kill. They will kill." He arrived from Germany, and he told this to my sister, and my sister believed him. He also spoke with my uncle. My uncle was a very educated man who suddenly, at the age of seventy, started to learn Latin, because he said that perhaps God does not speak Hebrew. He had such a broad political perception; when the Germans occupied Czechoslovakia, he said, "Idiots, why are you glad? Tomorrow it will happen here," and he had to escape the house, because he was a Polish anti-patriot. That is to say that he had a political perception, he understood. But somewhere he had some kind of a… blockage in his arteries—I don't know how else to call it… some sort of protection or illusion that clouded his mind. He said, "It can't be that they will kill people. It just cannot happen."

Ezra: Let's go back for a moment to your family's neighbors during those years. You said that people of the town felt close to one another, except for the hooligans who stood at the entrance to the shop, and whom your mother drove out with the yardstick that was reinforced with a layer of copper.

Dina: How do you know this?

Ezra: I know because those who used to come to Petah Tikva[22] to sell fabrics brought their yardsticks from Poland. The very same fellows. What happened to them, if you remember? When was there a turning point, if in fact a turning took place?

Dina: As I said earlier, the Jewish boys did not study in the *gymnasium*. And we girls, obviously would never date boys our own age, so we were three to four girls who usually went with Polish boys, because they attended the *gymnasium*. So, our young male friends were Polish, and they held one line, which was anti-German and pro-Jewish. They were all members of the underground. They all prepared themselves for the moment in which they would need to act. And they did, and later they left and went into the forests.

I will tell you for example about a friend of mine. They wanted to save her, but her parents did not agree. The Polish boyfriend of my girlfriend wanted to save her, but her mother said, "No, you are leaving with us," because she did not want to leave her in the hands of a Pole.

---

22 Petah Tikva—A town in the middle of Israel, where Ezra was born and raised.

In 1942, when searches were carried out in the Jewish houses, we used to hide at times in Polish houses. On one of these occasions, we gave our Polish neighbor our Torah, as well as the *chanukiah* that my father had inherited from his father. The *chanukiah* had been made in 1011, and the Torah was from 1012. When my mother returned after the war and asked this neighbor to return the items, she replied, "How come you returned? No one returned"—the very same neighbor who had lived next door to us. Years later, my brother Marek tried to purchase the *chanukiah* for a great deal of money, but did not succeed in returning it to our family.

Ezra: So, in this town, it did not happen the way it occurred in other towns, where suddenly the townspeople brought their knives out of the straw and said, "Now let's have you pay back for Jesus."

Dina: No. This was probably a town of a different kind.

The Escape from Koszyce

Dina: I'll tell you a story. A young Polish man by the name of Janek Mlynarczyk lived in Koszyce. He provided the inhabitants with coal for the winter months. The coal sacks were brought all the way to the houses, and Janek would load them onto a low window that was at the height of the street, and pour their contents into the cellar of the house. Every single year, with the arrival of winter, he used to come and ask how much coal we would need for that particular winter.

In the autumn of 1942, when Janek arrived to ask about the requested supplies for the coming winter, we had a young girl, four and a half years old, staying with us; Danushka was her name. She was staying with us along with her brother, Asher, and her mother, Hadassah, my mother's cousin. Avraham, Hadassah's husband, had gone with my father and brother, to Russia, and left her and the young children behind. The reason for this was that in Krakow, a ghetto was already formed up, and the earth had started to shake.

Danushka always played under a table, probably because this was safe. My mother said to Janek, "It would be good to have the regular quantity; the coming winter will be harsh; we might need more coal later and will not be able to find it; one never knows here with the new rules." And Danushka said from her hiding place under the table, "Buy lots of coal, so that the Germans will be warm." My mother did not pay attention to what the child said. So Janek asked, "What is she saying there about the Germans?" and again she said, "Buy a lot of coal so that the Germans will be warm." When they asked Danushka what she was talking about, she said, "You don't know, you will not be here. They will take us away, as they do in all the towns, so why are you buying coal?" She was four and a half years old… Janek looked at my mother and said to her, "You know what? I sometimes listen to children and think that they are much cleverer than we are. Let's think about what she is saying." At that moment, my sister entered the room. Later, they told me that Janck was very fond of her. I did not know that at the time. And he told her this story, what the child had said. And she said to him, "What do you propose? What do you think can be done? If we go, all of us, then this will be the end…" And she asked him, "Do you have any possibility in the underground, to arrange Arian certificates for us?" "Yes. If I am to receive two genuine birth certificates. Based on them, I could arrange it," he said.

That evening, my mother went to the town's priest. The priest had a woman and had children with her, and Mother knew about it; it was never a secret. He used to buy from us. There were times when he could afford to pay, and others when he would buy on credit. He used to play chess with my father, and so he was like one of the family. She went to the priest and said to him: "I need to save my two daughters. If you can give me two birth certificates, you will rescue me." He never asked a single question. He had two Polish girls who had gone willingly to work in Germany, and of course their birth certificates were in the church, and he gave her both. A few days later, Janek arranged two genuine certificates for my sister and me. In the certificates, Hanka was called Matilda Krzeczowska, and my name was Eugenia (Genia) Krzeczowska.

We could now travel across Poland with our new identities; two young girls without parents. Janek arranged for my mother a forged, and not genuine, certificate that had no background; that had no foundation. He also organized documents for my cousin, her two children and my aunt. He organized Arian documents for seven people. When he arranged the certificates, I arranged one for a Jewish friend of mine. I gave him as well a forged certificate, and so, altogether there were eight. My sister went as well to my uncle, who was in the *Judenrat*, and told him that she could arrange forged certificates for his children, but he said he would not send his children to a forced conversion from Judaism. They were fourteen and sixteen years old. "I have experienced war, The First World War; you did not," he said to her. "It was difficult, but we survived. We will survive this time as well. The worst that can happen is that they will send us to forced labor camps. After the war we will return, and I will have Jewish children rather than *goyim*." My sister said to him, "But we will not return; we will not survive, because these forced labor camps are concentration camps." But he said he did not believe that anything bad would happen.

Ezra: At that time, what motivated Janek? Was it natural that someone would come to the rescue?

Dina: No. it was not. But I will explain to you what happened. My sister was about three years older than me. Since my mother was greatly occupied with running the business, my sister was everything to me—she was a mother, she was a sister, she was a friend, she was a coach, she was a teacher. And you can understand it. When she could spare me from something, she would not involve me. She thought that I was at an age in which I had to be spared from things. There was no need to tell me everything. What one could avoid saying, one didn't have to say. She told me that we had certificates and that we were setting out to a personal battle; that is how she phrased it. We were not going out to a camp, we would have to fight for our survival on a daily basis. As I had received a certificate indicating that I was twenty-three years old, while I was nearly eighteen, she said, "You need to conduct a double battle. You will have to pass both as older and as Polish. These things will be tough." But she did not let on that this was going to be a life or death struggle. Her protection over me was complete. At the same time, I took for granted that someone had extended a helping hand, because I had so many Polish friends who had stretched their minds about how to help us and what to do with us. They refused to accept, as a matter of fact, that we had to leave.

An incident took place one day, and it was really like returning to life from death. It was said that the following day, all of the Jews would be expelled from the town. And so, Janek came that night and told us to go to the Polish cemetery and wait there until a certain hour. He would then come and take us across the Wisla by boat, and there he would find us a place to hide for the day. There was nothing I was afraid of more than this cemetery. And Janek did come to the cemetery, took us and crossed the Wisla with us. We were there, in a barn, for a day and a half, until we heard someone pass by, saying that they had not expelled the Jews. We then returned home for another three months. I remember that when I returned to the house, it no longer felt like my home. I felt more like I was arriving at a hotel. We knew that it could happen any moment. It was a period filled with happiness, while knowing that every single day could be the last. When each day passed, and they had not come for us, I did not take it for granted. I recall that, along with two of my girlfriends, we were in some kind of euphoria; we still slept in our own beds, and we could still eat and walk and take strolls; but as I said, it did not last for very long. And then came the real moment, and Janek carried out the same drill, but we never returned.

•

We knew of the target dates for the transports, because the Germans and their Polish aides had booked the carriages for the set dates in which they would herd together the Jews from our area for a transport.[23] The railway station was not located in our town. The

---

23 Transport is short for the Nazi usage of railways to transport the condemned prisoners from the Jewish Ghettos in Nazi-occupied Europe to selected extermination sites.

Jews were taken by carriages from Koszyce to the Germans' target destinations, from a collection point in Brzeko; a town larger than Koszyce.

This information helped my mother to plan our escape. Janek acted bravely in creating a rescue plan for my sister and me. He approached his business partner in Krakow and obtained his immediate help. The partner agreed to accommodate us, the two "Polish" girls who needed help in his house. My mother gave my Aunt Miriam the partner's address. Mother parted from us at home. I do not recall all the details of our parting, but I remember well that the fact that she did not come with us broke my heart.

With the forged certificates in our pockets, we left again, my sister and me, for the Polish cemetery. There, according to Janek's plan, was the safest place to hide. We waited a whole night in the grave-yard. Janek said that he could take us across to the other bank of the Wisla only during the dark hours. During that long evening in the cemetery, I was scared to death. When night fell, every rustle made us jump. My sister, who was concerned that I would feel her own fears, said to me, "You have no reason to fear the dead; the living are the ones who can cause us harm." Under the mantle of darkness, Janek succeeded to bring a small boat next to the banks of the Wisla, where he tied it in a hidden place and came to fetch us.

We hurried from the dark cemetery, through many trees and along an unfamiliar path that required the alertness of our senses in order not to fall into pits or bump into a cut-down tree trunk on our way to our destination—the boat on the Wisla. And thus, Janek brought us across the river in a vessel designed for two people.

The small suitcase we took with us contained only a few necessary things—one dress, a coat, a jacket and underwear. I remember that we took with us souvenirs, such as a brooch in the image of a cypress, and a small necklace, which were well hidden by being sewn into the buttons of our dresses. We did not take food. Janek gave us a non-kosher sausage, bread and water. After sailing for a few hours on the Wisla in complete darkness, Janek led us to the second bank and from there to Krakow, to the house of his partner, who had agreed to host us overnight.

Janek explained our arrival to his partner by saying that we were girls who were with the underground, "burnt" by informers and no longer able to walk in broad daylight. This was done in order not to raise the partner's suspicion, so that he would help in smuggling us. And it did help. The partner's wife received us in their house. She immediately arranged for us food and places to sleep. She served us red, hot and oily borscht,[24] which we did not like and tried to secretly avoid eating. In the end, we poured the soup into the stove that heated the room, and stayed famished the night through.

The plan was to stay a few days in their house, but this changed because my Aunt Miriam, who managed to escape the *aktion* that took place in Koszyce in the fall of 1942, arrived, taking us all by surprise, and completely turning the tables.

Mother, who had stayed in Koszyce after our departure, was one of the last Jews in the town. Two weeks after we had left, she traveled to Warsaw to an acquaintance, whose husband was the hairdresser of my cousin's children. The uncle of this hairdresser worked in the Ministry of Education, and she was able to stay with them for a while. Mother managed to inform my sister, via the postal services, about her place of residence.

•

---

24 Borscht is a soup of Ukrainian origin that is popular in many Eastern and Central European cuisines. In most traditional recipes, it is made with beetroot as the main ingredient.

Dina: They took the Jews of Koszyce. They took them to a place near the town. And they took them nowhere else. They placed them next to trees and finished them off, one after the other. There is evidence to that effect because Miriam, my aunt, my mother's sister, came from there, and succeeded in escaping to Krakow, to the address she knew we were at. This was a very tragic episode.

When Janek had taken us from home and brought us to Krakow to his friend, who also worked in the coal business, he told him that he had with him two Polish girls who had escaped due to political persecution and needed a shelter for some time. We arrived there, started to converse with his wife, and she loved us very much. But when my aunt came, the wife realized who we really were, but was afraid that her husband did not know. We did not wish to create a conflict in the family, and so we said, "You know what? We will go away, just don't say a word to your husband." But she then said, "No. I will not let you leave. You are Jewish, and I need to look after you. I will go to my husband." And then she went and told him, and we stayed there a few days, but later it turned out that the place was no longer a refuge, because the Jewish man for whom I arranged Arian certificates needed money and informed on us, and we had to run away from there.

Ezra: How do you know that it was him?

Dina: Because they told us later. He also took money from us in order to exchange it into smaller notes, but never returned it. From there we went to two women who said that they could arrange, against payment, a place in Stalowa Wola.

Stalowa Wola

Dina: In Stalowa Wola there was a factory. Before the war, Jews were not allowed to work there. It was a relatively new town, with a weapons factory, with all the hierarchy of workers, foremen and engineers. Each of them had their own neighborhood. And there was a man there named Oliaczek who was prepared, for money, to arrange for us jobs, as well as accommodations. We paid him at such an exorbitant ratio that if, let's say, he earned 300 a month, we paid him 3,000 a month for a place to work and a place to stay.

Ezra: He arranged everything, thinking that you were Poles in every respect, and he did not know.

Dina: No. Of course he knew. He knew, and he lived with a woman outside matrimony, and she was one of the women who brought us there. We were there for quite a long time. We worked there for almost one year.

Ezra: When did this take place?

Dina: in 1942-1943.

•

A Chance Meeting on a Train

Dina: There is something amusing and coincidental that happened on one of the occasions of my travels from Stalowa Wola to Warsaw to meet my mother, because sometimes they had to change Mother's place of residence.

Ezra: Your mother also portrayed herself as Polish.

Dina: She portrayed herself as a deaf and dumb woman—a Polish lady, but one who could not speak, so that no one would hear her accent. She did not have a good Polish accent, because the first intonation she heard at home had been that of Yiddish. And then it accompanies you all your life. She was concealed with the help of a certificate, in case they came searching, but she did not speak. I traveled by myself on the train to Warsaw, and a young man sitting across from me attempted to open a conversation. During this whole time, it had never occurred to me that someone would come out and talk to me, because I was a young girl. I was always under the impression that if someone wanted to talk, they already knew something about me, or would soon discover. So, the less one spoke, the better. I read a book and didn't talk. But the journey took hours—it was a five-hour trip. So, it was impossible not to talk the entire time. So he offered me something; I didn't smoke, I wasn't hungry. Nothing. He asked me about the book I was reading, and I needed to reply. Slowly slowly, a conversation developed. He introduced himself as Zbigniew Krzeczowski, and my surname in my Polish certificates was Krzeczowska. In response to his question, I muttered some kind of name... Genia, I answered. But he insisted and continued asking, while saying that he had not heard well my name. For lack of any option, I repeated my name, Genia Krzeczowska. The young man was delighted with the discovery. This coincidence gladdened him very much, while I was close to fainting. He asked me about my place of birth, and I told him the name of the village where I was "born," and it turns out that he was, in actual fact, a "true cousin of mine," and knew the history of the family. And he said that six years ago he had attended the wedding of another cousin in his hometown, but could not remember me at all. And I told him, "what six years can do..." and I understood that I was in a great jeopardy, because if he continued to ask, then I was done. But there is an unyielding defense mechanism that gets activated inside us. I took my bag— I also had a suitcase, but I left it there—and I said that I was going for a moment to the toilet, and at the first available opportunity, I left the train and took the next one after a few hours. From all of the millions of people, I had to meet him.

•

Dina: In Stalowa Wola, we were working in the lion's den, because there was an underground located there, which was responsible for provocations. The Germans stood there on guard. Once I was working the night shift, I had Jewish workers, and they spoke amongst themselves in Yiddish, saying: "We don't know why this Pole treats us so well." I used to give them permission to rest on top of the stoves. They had to finish their work quotas. I used to tell them, "Work faster, go to rest, and then come back." I also used to bring them bread and just leave it around. I did not tell them to take it, because I was not allowed to do that, but they got the hint.

We had in the factory a German foreman, whose name was Zurik. He used to walk around with his dog beside him, and both became the terror of the factory. Everyone was afraid of him, and they called him "The Hangman." On one occasion, when I was in charge of the shift and allowed the Jews to rest a bit, he came to me to ask about the whereabouts of the Jews. I then explained to him that if they rested, they worked better. I don't know if he bought into this, but later he used to come around a lot, to watch what I was doing.

One night he told me that the Ukrainians[25] had caught two Jewish women working in the factory under assumed identities and hanged them at the entrance to the factory. "Who knows how many more of them are here?" he said. I used to leave work at seven o'clock in the morning and would see my sister arriving, because she worked the morning shifts. She worked in the office, and I worked outside, on the manufacturing floor. So at the end of my shift that night, I thought to myself, "What do I do?" If I had met her on the way and told her not to go inside, then we would have needed to escape on the very same day, because they would immediately send someone out to see what had happened. Unless you had in your possession a note from a doctor; you could not just get up and go; it was like the military there. We would have also endangered the man who gave us the jobs.

I knew that if I did not meet her, then it would be a day filled with danger; certainly seeing those corpses above your head when you pass through was not a very pleasant scene; especially when in your head the foreman's words regarding who knows how many more like this there are, kept echoing.

I did not meet my sister. She must have entered beforehand. I reached our house, and for an entire day, I needed to wait and wonder if anything had happened to her. I had no way

25 The original reasons for the Ukrainian collaboration with the Nazi regime—included Ukrainian political aspirations for regaining independence, and resurgent nationalism, but also widespread anger and resentment against the Russians over the genocide by famine engineered in Soviet Ukraine only a few years earlier. These sentiments were coupled with general resentment towards other ethnic groups (such as Jews, Tatars, Roma people, and Poles) as well as the ancient notions of anti-Semitism.

of entering the factory, and there was also no point in doing so. I recall that when she finally returned home, I was not sure how to take it. In the end, I regarded it as a temporary gift from God. And then we were sitting and debating with Oliaczek about what to do. We knew that we had to escape that night. We moved our stuff to the neighbor, Stermakova, who knew that we were Jewish, though we had never discussed it with her. She was a Polish lady, simply out of this world and she loved us. And this is something I must emphasize—they say that there is luck in the world, but this is not to do with luck; it's to do with personality. And it's not that I want to pride myself, but wherever I went, I knew how to create for myself conditions that caused people to love me, and that was crucial. We brought all the things to her, whatever we could. We also gave a lot of money to that man—Oliaczek. We could not all stay together in the same place—it was too dangerous. So Hanka and I decided to go to Warsaw, without knowing exactly where. We knew that Mother had stayed in a hideout in Warsaw, together with my aunt.

Ezra: Please go on and tell about this neighbor.

Dina: The neighbors did not like this Oliaczek, this man. He was really a terrible person. Earlier on, Vanda, the woman who had lived with him, broke up with him and ran away, and we stayed. He loved to drink. When he got drunk, he used to walk in the streets and say that he had two Jewish women in his house. We saw that this was dangerous, and Stermakova, the neighbor, told us that the fact that Oliaczek was getting drunk out on the streets was dangerous. But what could we do? He had to drink until he got drunk, because this was his nature. He started drinking in the house, and we drank together with him. Stermakova used to arrive together with her husband, and we would all drink together. But we did not actually drink; we only pretended to. But the very fact of staying in the house, together with a drunkard, was very unpleasant.

But still, before this, I must say something about Janek. Janek, the one who arranged the certificates for us, did not abandon us; he did not just send us across the water, and leave us to our fate; he accompanied us. And since we did not have anywhere to go during the holidays, and since it was impossible for two girls to be somewhere and not go home for the holidays, we invented a story that our parents had been killed and that we were on our own. You know, you invent all sorts of stories, and you don't want to become friends with anyone, because if you have friends, you need to tell, and then you need to lie, and then you need to remember the lies. And my sister suddenly acquired a friend who was of Russian origin, and his name was Panes. He was an engineer, and he escaped with his family to Poland during the war.

I cannot explain intuition to you. He said to my sister that the name Matilda did not suit her at all and that he would call her Hanka. I am confident that he did not know that this is her true name, because he did not know her. Anyway, we told him what was going on, and he helped us a lot. For someone who knew our secret, he understood how to behave. He told all sorts of people that he knew our family. Janek saw to it that we would not be isolated because people in a town like this are very bored, and boredom is a terrible thing for someone who has something to hide, because you walk down the street, and people start talking about you: "What are they doing here, these two young women; they don't have any friends, they never go home." Anyhow, Janek started visiting with another of his friends, who was blond with a kind of a mustache. They came to visit regularly to create some sort of a foursome. And we used to walk down the street and do all sorts of demonstrations of friendship, so that people would see that we had friends and that this no doubt was the reason for us not traveling home. In any case, when we had to go to Warsaw, we only had one address to go to.

Ezra: At that time, there were already no doubts regarding what was happening?

Dina: Yes. We knew exactly. Also because the Jews I worked with spoke openly amongst themselves; they did not know that I understood what they were saying. We knew that the Germans were killing Polish people as well. And that the Polish underground had already started to suffer losses. We knew explicitly what was happening. We did not know what the intensity or the methods were. But we knew that they were murdering. Also, my aunt told us that they had killed everyone; that they had annihilated the Jews of Koszyce before they reached any destination.

Ezra: What went through your minds? It was as if you were standing in the bleachers, watching all that was happening. How did you feel? What was going on inside you?

Dina: You know, this is not all of it. I was in Rozwadow, a town located near Stalowa Wola. I happened to be there when the Jews were forced out of their houses, and I saw it. I think that it can be said that I am perhaps one of the very few Jewish women who watched it as if watching a movie. Because I did not participate in it, and this is something I shall never forget. Because there was much disparagement there, and the wild laughter of the Germans, and the sense that this was some sort of a game. They told the Jews to bring out all of their warm, down blankets, and then they shot the blankets, and the feathers began to fly around, making it look like snow. It was horrific. This was not an ordered removal from the houses. This was a game. They let their soldiers enjoy "the game." You are asking how this influenced us?

Ezra: You were actually watching everything parade in front of you as if in a movie. And you are this young Polish woman who stands there and watches, but at your core, you are what is called, "*Di Yiddishe Tochter*" (the Jewish daughter).

Dina: You find yourself in a labyrinth of feelings, and you have no idea what the next day will bring. You are blocked. You walk the path because you have no idea how life will continue. I once convinced myself not to suffer too much, because I did not know what would happen the following day. I decided to live the day, at least most of the hours and minutes, in the best way that I could—because I didn't know what would happen tomorrow, and I really had no idea what the next day would look like.

The Escape to Warsaw

Dina: I want to tell you something about fate. When we decided to go to Warsaw, we took the midnight train. It was dangerous, because you could not travel without a reason, and you needed a certificate indicating that you are on leave or something, but we just took off; we had nothing to lose. Just before we got on the train, we caught a glimpse of Zourik's dog. The same dog I used to see at the factory. After the train started moving, we saw Zourik, and later it became apparent that he, too, had seen us. The following day, we saw in the newspaper that they were searching for two girls with our names, whose details matched those of our certificates. We had to change our certificates immediately because we had escaped a military factory and actually fled the army without permission.

•

Once, after the war had ended, and we were free, I was standing in a queue for bread, when suddenly I saw Zourik's familiar figure; a figure I would have recognized from miles away. The man was engraved in my memory. I regarded him as a monster. I left the queue and started to walk in a different direction. He caught up with me and put a hand on my shoulder. He was a *Volksdeutsche* by origin and spoke both languages: Polish and German. He approached me and said bluntly and without any introduction: "Idiot, if I wanted to be done with you, I could have easily done it then." He then pushed towards me a note that had his name and address on it, and said: "Remember who kept you alive." This was the last time I met him. The feeling was that the angel of death had returned to my life. This time, that angel of death requested—so it said in the note—that I speak in his favour should he have to face trial… and after he disappeared, I remained hurting and dumbfounded. I returned to our place of residence, where my sister was waiting for me. My face disclosed my feelings. I told her what had happened in the bread queue, and we chose not to do anything about it. The man who had acted as a human monster towards other people, innocent people, wanted to receive a positive character reference from any survivor who had had the misfortune of being in his presence. We had no intention of offering him help of any sort.

•

Dina: We had one address in Warsaw. The address of Zosia Stefkova, who lived on 139 Marszalkowska Street. How did we come to know her? Aunt Sarah, my mother's sister, lived not too far from 139 Marszalkowska Street. When she and her family were sent to the Ghetto, she wrote to us saying that we could mail parcels to the address of her friend, Zosia Stefkova, who was Polish and who had agreed to forward the parcels to my aunt. Until 1942, we sent packets to both Aunt Sarah and her family, and to Stefkova, because we knew that she too had found herself in difficulty. In the packets, we put sugar, flour and legumes from our house in Koszyce, because we still had those supplies at the time.

When we arrived, my sister and I, at Stefkova's, it was a harsh and cold winter. She lived on the sixth floor of a house that had been bombed by the Germans as part of the bombing of Warsaw. She occupied one room together with her daughter and husband, as well as a small dog. This was an unusual barking dog. The toilets were outside this room. She did not have room for us. But Stefkova had such a special quality that it was indescribable (after the war had ended, we understood that Stefkova was, as well, a member of the Polish underground). She was a simple woman, whose husband worked as a doorman at an educational institute. This is a long story, because he had a brother in Busko-Zdrój, where another of my mother's sisters used to live. And so, they were close to the family. She led us to one of the bombed rooms in an apartment that had no roof. There was a bed there and warm blankets and an umbrella, but the following morning, we woke up covered in snow. And what could they do with us? We could not stay in this room. To begin with, she made contact with members of the underground, and they arranged for us alternative certificates. From that moment on, my name was Genowefa Lubowidzka, leaving behind Genia Krzeczowska.

Ezra: And the Polish underground arranged things for two Jewish girls or for two Polish girls?

Dina: I can't even say. What she said to them, I don't know. These were not genuine certificates; they had no real background. If we had been caught, then it would have been bad news for us.

Ezra: In 1943, the Warsaw Ghetto Uprising begins.[26]

Dina: And I am watching it from afar.

Ezra: And what happens? The Warsaw Ghetto Uprising, the Poles, the Jews, everything bursts into flames. Can you go back for a moment to the Warsaw Ghetto Uprising?

---

26 On April 19, 1943, on the eve of the Jewish Holiday, Passover, the *aktion* of extermination of the Warsaw Ghetto began, and the underground organizations reacted with resistance. The Germans were surprised by the demonstration of resistance and by the fact that the residents of the Ghetto hid in bunkers and other places of hiding. After five days of fighting, the Germans began in a systematic way to set fire to the Ghetto houses, and the Ghetto became a fire trap for its inhabitants. For over a month, the Jews of the Ghetto fought bravely. This was the first civil uprising that took place inside a city in Nazi-occupied Europe. For further reading about The Warsaw Ghetto Uprising please see the appendix entitled, "Warsaw Ghetto."

Dina: The Warsaw Ghetto Uprising was for us, to begin with, a "shot in the arm" that said not everything was lost. We did not know what the magnitude was, and we did not know what was happening there. We were on Kolska Street. I stood on the roof with a Polish lady friend, and we saw how the houses burnt, and how people jumped out of the houses. My Polish friend, who was an educated lady from Poznan, said that this was the most beautiful sight she had ever seen in her life. I had a strong desire to give her a light shove and have her fall from that roof. I did not reply and turned away from her, because I had tears in my eyes, and could not cry openly. I came down from the roof, and then I understood that there are people who are really sick in their minds. Truly so. If anyone could see something like this and then say that it was the most beautiful sight they had ever laid their eyes upon, then what else could you expect from them? You know, this was such a terrible realization that it continues to have its influence on me until now, to this very moment.

Ezra: You had encounters of a different nature?

Dina: I had had encounters with people who helped me, and in an unexpected way, she, whom I liked and who was my friend, to hear her suddenly saying something like this—my world simply fell apart. I also heard that Jews were escaping via the sewage pipes and that there were many Poles who would not let them come out. And I asked about it, and they said that it was true. I had no personal contact with this, since I did not have to escape from the Ghetto.

Ezra: I am asking about this contact on the inside. The rumour in Poland probably was that the Jews were being taken to their death. However, here, the Jews were rebelling. Was there time to think that perhaps this was another kind of death? This time, rising against the Germans, killing the Germans so that they know that the Jews also know how to fight. Did it cross your mind? After all, all of this was taking place within a short period of time. The whole city was facing, and the underground was facing, this horror, and no help was being offered. On the contrary, they were blocking the sewage pipelines.

Dina: There were those who pointed out the fact that the Poles sent ammunition and helped. And I was part of a group of people who helped me too, and who never mentioned a word about it. We know about it in retrospect. We did not know it then.

Ezra: I am inquiring about then, about you, the Jewish girl.

Dina: At the time, I understood that the Polish underground helped people who came via the gutters. However, then, on that roof, something else ended, and that was some kind of a powerful projector shedding light on the Polish people. On what they were like and how they actually felt. That there might have been a very small group of individuals who were helping, but that most people identified with the majority.

Ezra: In the coil that was etched in your brain at that time, was there already a record indicating the enormity of the millions who were going to their death?

Dina: You cannot think like this. You live more like an animal. You do not read a newspaper. There was no newspaper. You do not hear the news. You are like a chased animal, you yourself. You live in such a limited way. You want another day to pass, and another day, and to push time forward. You are hurting so much, and the whole time, you question yourself if you are treating those around you well. I always had a feeling that, perhaps, I neglected Mother; maybe she was suffering? Perhaps she longed for something? Perhaps I was seeing daylight, whereas she did not get to see the sunlight. Do you understand?

•

Hanka is by herself in Krakow

At a certain point, Hanka moved to Krakow by herself, and there she started feverishly to buy and sell everything she could. She had a great sense for commerce, which was seasoned with a sense of practicality. She knew what was needed for us to have means for survival when we would meet again. She started collecting as much money as possible—above and beyond her daily needs for survival. In fact, she had begun to do it earlier, back in our house in Koszyce, where she sold various things and earned money. She even managed to sell our furniture for considerable amounts of money.

The money she earned from selling things, Hanka was meant to hide until it became needed. She found an original way to do it, and prepared cloth-covered buttons, and hid the money inside them. She used to walk around in the market and became a known figure to anyone who wished to sell anything. In this way, she collected considerable assets—from half dollars to diamonds of various sizes. I recall from her stories how she used to prepare by herself buttons of different sizes that contained gold coins and diamonds, and she then fastened them to dresses in a way that would hide them from everyone.

A few months later, Hanka returned to Warsaw. Warsaw was divided at the time into regions. Certain areas had been conquered earlier on. Hanka's area had been occupied a long time before mine.

•

Life in a Birdcage

From Dina's conversation with Ezra:

Dina: Stefkova arranged a place for me to stay with a divorcee who lived near Warsaw. She worked as an engineer in Warsaw, and had a son called Vazik, but no one to look after him. For my sister, she arranged a small place with Polish underground people, who agreed to host her. I started to take care of the child. I had no idea how to cook. My flops at the beginning are hard to describe. I lived there in a bird-cage. The engineer's father had once been an actor. After his retirement, he transferred his love for acting to birds, and he had in the cage hundreds of canaries and other birds. Since there was no other space, I lived in this room. This child became unusually attached to me. His mother was probably not mentally stable, and in any case, she began to suspect that I was her ex-husband's lover and that he had arranged for me to stay in her house in order for me to steal the child's love and then to take the child with me and leave. This was so far from the truth—to conceive such an idea… I did not know how a person could be so unaware of someone else's situation, how she could even begin to think of me in such a manner. Anyhow, one fine day, her ex-husband arrived, and I told him this story.

Ezra: When does this take place?

Dina: In 1944.

Ezra: In 1943 you moved to Warsaw?

Dina: Yes. So when her ex-husband came to visit me, we sat together, and I told him about how much I suffered there, about the plots she was conspiring and of what she accused me. There were times when I simply could not get away from her, and he sat and caressed me like this, and said, "Never mind, the war will soon end, and all will be well, and you will be able to return home, and you will have a family of your own, and you will not have to suffer unbalanced women." At that moment, the woman appeared. She had returned earlier than scheduled; I do not know, some kind of feminine instinct of hers, and she saw that he was caressing me and comforting me. And she said, "Now I've caught you; you are to leave this house, you will not stay here for another moment."

So then I traveled to Warsaw to the only address I had, Stefkova's address, because I did not want to reach my sister's address; she had a small part of a sofa at someone's house, and I did not want to burden her. I only let her know that I had lost my place. We met before 5 pm by the PKO Bank in Warsaw, and she told me that she would arrive later to take me from Stefkova's place and that she would arrange something. We took leave of each other at 5 pm, and the Polish uprising began at five minutes past five. I did not manage to reach Stefkova's place, and the next time I saw my sister was after the war.

The Polish Uprising

On that day, August 2nd, 1944, exactly when I bid my sister farewell after meeting with her in the bank's lobby, the Polish uprising[27] began. This was one of the most difficult periods in my life, and it is still difficult for me to speak about it.

After the initial success of the uprising, which surprised the Germans very much, a counterattack began. The Germans bombed the Poles with all sorts of weapons. We nicknamed the sound of one of the cannons, "*krowa*" (cow). These guns were placed on wagons and moved all across Warsaw. Any senior resident of Warsaw will be familiar with what I mention here. The "cow" was dangerous because it fired six shells in one go, and we had no means of protection from it. One time I hid in an underground station that had a staircase leading to a public shelter where I could hide and even sleep. One compassionate woman gave me a bag filled with dry rice, and I ate it for a period that seemed like an eternity.

Very often, we came out looking for something edible. We called these scouting operations "crumb hunting." At those times, the houses were left unlocked. People knew that locking the doors of houses that remained erect would result in someone breaking in, removing the doors in one way or another and robbing everything. They, therefore, chose to keep their few belongings and what little food they had, and to keep the doors open for anyone passing.

German snipers were hiding on rooftops and they shot at the people passing by, especially while crossing the road. In one of the times that I had to cross the road, a sniper shot at me. Blood covered me, and upon my arrival at the shelter, they washed me but could not

---

27 For further reading about the Polish uprising in Warsaw Please see the appendix entitled, "The Polish Uprising."

find the source of the blood. In the end, it turned out that I was not the one who got hurt, but someone else, a man passing near me.

The days of bombing during the Polish uprising seemed endless to me. Later, I found out that they had lasted 63 consecutive days. During this time, nearly a quarter of a million people were killed in Warsaw, and approximately 60% of the houses in the city were demolished. Those days left in me extremely traumatic scars that I could not perceive at the time, because I was thoroughly occupied with the day-to-day survival. All of this led to my agoraphobia, my fear of open spaces, which was my post-trauma psychological response to the horrific situation I was in. In the years to come, it would reappear as a fear of something as simple as crossing a street.

From Dina's conversation with Ezra:

Dina: During the Polish uprising that took place in 1944, I am completely on my own. Really, and absolutely, on my own and alone, for nine weeks in this hell.

Ezra: And where do you go?

Dina: I am on the street. I see that they begin to shoot. I enter a house and stay in a doorway for a while. I am alone. I am utterly alone and do not have anyone at my side. I know my mother's address in Warsaw; it is very far, and I cannot get there while they are shooting. I know my sister's address, but meanwhile, there is a border there; the Germans have occupied the place, and here the Poles are fighting, and I am on the Polish side the entire time. Moreover, I am wandering together with the fighting Poles for nine weeks, from street to street.

Ezra: What do you do there?

Dina: I don't do anything.

Ezra: Wherever they move, you move with them?

Dina: Yes.

Ezra: Where do you sleep, and what do you eat?

Dina: I sleep in basements. I barely eat. I eat just rice, and here and there when people leave something. It is hard to explain it to anyone who was not there, because the Germans had this kind of method—to conquer one street after the other, to demolish it and to move on. So everyone from the same street ran under the houses, because they were connected one to another under the ground, and this way you could move from house to house. And there was also the Polish army, the A.K.[28], those who fought, and the population. The civilians moved with the army, and later it was difficult to differentiate between them. They wore a ribbon of some kind. With this flow of movement, everyone found themselves eventually in a place from which there was no escape. The Germans pulled everyone out like mice and sent them to Germany to forced labor camps.

Now I will tell a bit about myself.

During this process of running from place to place, I decided at a certain moment that there was nothing to lose. I would walk up to the nicest apartment, where I would sit and indulge myself. Because the houses were empty, and there was no one there. Those who could flee, and those who could not, did not stay in the apartments, because this was dangerous. Everything was bombed. Each time they

---

28 The A.K., Armia Krajowa—the Polish underground forces that operated during the Nazi occupation and were active all over Poland from the collapse of the regular Polish army in 1939 until the occupation of Poland by the Red Army in January 1945. Most of the fighting against the Nazis in occupied Poland was carried out by the Armia Krajowa.

would bomb a different neighborhood, until they demolished everything.

I climbed to a beautiful apartment that was filled with lots of
fine China and comfortable sofas. There was one sofa there,
a lovers' sofa they call it, with two seats where it is possible
to look at each other like this, and I sat on this couch and
thought that if a lovely young man would have been there
with me, it would have been nice. Suddenly a girl entered.
I looked at her, and immediately saw that she was Jewish.
The door had been open, and most probably she had felt the
same wish to be, for a little while, in a "normal" situation—
not to be amidst these ruins and dirt. And we stared at one
another, and she said, "You" and I said, "You." And we no
longer feared anything; it was nearly the end. I knew that
perhaps I could last for another day. How long can a person
hold on in such a situation? Also, I did not have anything
to eat. I had this bag of rice, and I ate out of it, pecking
like a bird. To begin with, we kissed and hugged, and this
was so warm. Suddenly, you know, it was so good. And we
sat down on the sofa, and I told her that a minute earlier
I had dreamt that a boy would come along, and now I was
so happy that it was her. I have a photograph of her. She was
my age, a beautiful girl, and she began to tell me the story
of her life and what she had gone through. She had stayed
with a wealthy family as a maid. The family fled, and she
had nowhere to go. She was scared that if she escaped with
them, she would be identified as a Jew. And so we sat in this
fashion on the sofa, and outside there was heavy shelling,
and we did not go downstairs… and suddenly the house
collapsed, and we fell together, on the couch, and nothing
happened to us. We fell down a few stories, got up from the
sofa, and came out as if all was as usual… Simply a story out

of this world. The house collapsed in a very gentle way, and we continued to sit on the sofa.

Ezra: I am not inquiring, only imagining…

Dina: Later, we did not need the stairs; some kind of a hill had formed up and we crossed it. I then lost this girl during the constant running around in Warsaw. I lost her, and I felt that I had lost the dearest sister. Up until today, I do not forgive myself. How could we lose one another?

Ezra: Did you try over the years to locate her?

Dina: I tried. Wherever I went, later in Warsaw, I always saw her somehow—part of her profile, part of her hair; I always ran after women thinking they were her, but only a part of her was there with all these women. None of them were her.

Ezra: And this is a story that's impossible to leave behind.

Dina: No, it is impossible to part with it because it was so much… this experience was special not only because she was Jewish but because she had a personality; she was very close to me. This was an extraordinary young woman. Perhaps she was a bit older than me, because I had become used to thinking that I was twenty-three years old, but she was probably about twenty-two years old, and I was actually twenty years old.

Ezra: It is hard to part with her, but let us move on.

Dina: Later, I was imprisoned in the cellar of a house that had completely collapsed. It was totally dark. There was nothing; you could not see anything; we were buried under the ruins. The Poles there started to pray, and this was the first time I had encountered a certain death, and I thought to myself that I will not pray. I believed that if I prayed now, I would betray myself and be untrue to myself, because I was not a believer; and so I did not pray.

Ezra: Did you have the strength to think?

Dina: I had the strength because my sister had continuously etched in my head, in my soul, that mere survival is not enough. You have to survive with your character, and with self-dignity, so you can look at yourself in the mirror. And one of the things she pointed out was in regards to the attitude towards men; she told me that we could survive the war in a much easier way if we lowered our standard. This depended on our decision regarding what we did for ourselves, and we decided that as long as we could save ourselves in a reasonable way and without lowering our life standard—not standard in terms of luxury, but rather the rules of life itself—we would do that, and that was the decision. For example, my sister, while we stayed in Warsaw for a period, saw to it that I received piano and English lessons so that after the war I would not be ignorant. And so, in terms of the belief in God, this was one of the principles; not to change my standpoint according to the circumstances—if I am a non-believer, then I am a non-believer, and I do not have to succumb in a moment of weakness to prayers and to the wrong belief.

Ezra: This means that you did not even experience anger at God. You did not have an object for anger.

Dina: No. I did not have an object for my anger. This was never my outlook. My worldview, as much as I was a young girl, was always that something had been created here, but that it has no pertinence, and it did not owe me anything, and I too, did not owe it much. If I owed anything, it would be only to nature, but not to someone or something that had created it.

In any case, I did not have an address; I did not have anyone to turn to. The Poles sat there and rolled their beads and prayed. Moreover, I thought about how the best thing to do was to rescue what I had. First, I wetted a handkerchief and put it in my mouth, so that all of this dust would not enter, and started to search for an opening out of this place. They were busy praying, and I was busy searching. And believe me, sometimes even one person can find rescue. There were perhaps 300 people in the cellar. I started searching, and I started urging others to begin to dig. We dug with our hands and we got out of there, and the proof is that I am here today.

At a certain point, I found my mother, who was with my aunt and with a small girl, who was five years old. My mother said to me, "Go be by yourself, don't cling to us; the moment you cling to us, we will all be gone, because in a group like this, we will all be immediately suspected. Together, we look more Jewish than when we are each one by herself." Apart from this, she said, "We will be like shackles on your legs. Run away, do something with your-self, by yourself, you will be able to; whereas together with us, you will not be able to." I willingly listened to her advice because this is how I wanted it, but it haunted me for quite a long time until I managed to get rid of my guilt feelings, which said that I needed, in fact, to stay with her and help her, though how or in what, I have no idea. In fact, they later found some sort of a place that had dried fruit. They lay on the sacks and did not know what was in them, but the smell was very sharp. They opened the bags and found the dried fruit, and they lived on them the whole time they were in Warsaw.

Ezra: How long was that?

Dina: Three weeks. They could take out of the sacks. But I did not have it; I only had a bag of rice.

Ezra: And you are with this one bag of rice that sustained you for a few weeks during this upheaval of the uprising.

Dina: I arrive at a place, and there was an old automobile and inside the automobile we hid, because this was safer than going around for no reason. And inside this car, someone lost his mind.

Ezra: Who are 'we'?

Dina: Just people I did not know.

Ezra: And you call them 'we'.

Dina: Because these were human beings.

Ezra: Some kind of a shared destiny.

Dina: Yes. And one of them went crazy and said that he had started the car and seemingly was driving it. And this was a scene in which I thought that if we were to stay there for an extended period, we would all lose our minds, because really, there was nothing to eat, there was nothing to drink. I realized that it is possible not to eat, you know, for a few weeks, and that if you nibble something here or there, you stay alive. Once we saw a dead horse, and someone took a piece of meat off it, made a small fire, put the piece of meat on it, arranged some kind of a long stick with a piece of rope in order to turn the meat from afar, because there were German snipers who only waited for the opportunity of someone coming out with a view to nailing him down. So we were waiting for the meat to be ready; the smell reached us, and at the very last moment, when we thought that the meat was ready, the snipers began shooting and ruined the meat and everything… and so you realize that this was also a game. And at a certain moment, they find us, all of us.

There was also a very tragic moment with the Russians. We reached the Wisla, and we heard that on the other bank there were Poles standing amongst the Russian troops and they wanted to help. It was cold, and one of those Polish soldiers swam across the Wisla and then swam back to report on our situation. So the Russians sent a few Polish soldiers, very few who didn't know how to carry on in urban combat, and they were killed like flies. And the Russian cannons were aimed, and not by accident, at us and not at the Germans. And so we called out to them and sent messengers, and they said it was a mistake, but they did not correct it. Later, in the history books, it was written that this was done on purpose, that they wanted the Poles to be annihilated together with the Germans, so that there would be no national Polish underground that would claim Poland for itself. So this hope vanished as well, and when the Germans arrived, they gathered all the Poles who were still around, and loaded us on trucks.

I had a green leather coat that I had been wearing the entire time and a white bag made of cloth, in which I put a few first aid items and the bag of rice. I also found a thin blanket that I put inside the bag, as well as more stuff that I added just so that the bag would have more weight. When I think now about the essence of this bag, I regard it as something that tied me to the ground, so that I would not be too light. The loneliness was so horrific; I was so alone with no one who knew what I was going through, that it made me fear that I would suddenly fly away, and the bag was something that added weight, enabling me to have some kind of weight on this ground.

The Germans saw the green coat and liked it very much. So the first thing they did was take it from me, and I was left without a jacket. I had a ring on one of my fingers; my hands were swollen, and they wanted the ring, and I could not take it off, and the German was about to cut my finger off. At the very last moment, I put my finger inside my mouth and began to suck it powerfully, and finally managed to take it off.

We were called to stand in a formation before they sent us in train cars to a place that used to be a factory in Plaszow near Warsaw. They were probably feeling, already in 1944, that the situation was getting worse, so they had transported to Germany the machines from this mill. And so we arrived at an empty factory. Before transporting us, they took our certificates. They ordered us, the women, into a line; a German officer approached us and said, "You see, I only have nine fingers. One of my fingers was cut off by a woman, a member of the underground, and now I shoot every tenth woman because of this finger." This is what he explained. We sat down, and he started counting. I was the eighth. Then came the ninth, and then the tenth, "*traach.*" Each time, the tenth was shot down, just like that. You looked at the line and thought to yourself, I could have been the tenth, and you stopped caring about anything. It was like some kind of a blurring of the brain and the soul.

However, what was most inconceivable was that the same officer saw me later, wobbling because of my weakness. He took me and said that he would bring me to a cellar where the military kitchen was located. He brought me to this basement and told the cook to give me food, but to do it very slowly, because my stomach was very sensitive. He told the cook to give me tea first, then semolina porridge and then a piece of bread, and also put some food in my white bag for the road. I ate and could not free myself from amazement: on the one hand, he killed every tenth woman, and on the other hand, he was so concerned, and in such a gentle way, about my stomach. How can one put these two things together? Later, he came over and said, "You know, why should you go to Germany to do this kind of work? Stay here, in Warsaw. We have furs the likes of which you never saw in your life. In the rooms we use, we have so much luxury and so many beautiful things." I looked at him and said that if I had stayed alive until now, and after such hardships, a fur was no longer impressive, and I would, therefore, go to the forced labor camp. I said, "You will find here many women who would want to accept your offer. Why me?" He did not argue with me.

I arrived in Plaszow. All of my worldly belongings now included that small bag and the blanket that I carried with me anywhere I went. There was an old factory there, from which they had removed all the machines, so that only large bolts now remained on the concrete. I put this blanket on the ground between four bolts to mark my territory and wept for three whole days. I suddenly realized that I was on my own, alone in this whole wide world. No one from my family knew where I was, and I did not have any idea where they were. The feeling of loneliness hit me so strongly that I started crying. Suddenly, all the horrors of the war, the fear of death and the horrible uncertainties I had lived through on a daily basis, they all rose up in me in a cry that lasted for three whole days. I could not stop the tears and could not do anything else but cry.

These were three foundational days for me. When the crying stopped, I decided to stop feeling sorry for myself. A few women sat next to me, and none of them looked at the other. Everyone was introspective. Nothing was surprising—for someone to cry for three whole days; for another to sit this way or lie that way. Everyone was in a kind of deep coma of their soul.

Ezra: During those three days, was there a moment when you wished to die?

Dina: Never. Never. The tears were some kind of purification; some kind of soul purification because I could not take it anymore. I was feeling so sad; when would it end—what was happening there.

The Forced Labor Camp

I was sent together with other women to a military labor camp in Germany. Anyone who had an opportunity to jump off the trains that were going to Germany did so and hid amongst the Poles. The rest of the people, those who stayed on the trains, were those who had no relatives in the Polish villages and towns and therefore became forced workers in the factories.

They sent us to Oschersleben, a town that had a plant for arms manufacturing with a residence area annexed to it. The camp was divided into a larger area, where the factory for ammunition was located, and a smaller area, where the prisoners who were performing temporary jobs were held. After a few months in the smaller camp, my division was sent back to the larger camp.

When I travel back in my mind to those hard days of forced labor in the camp, various memories come up, amongst them the constant hunger and the lack of sleep. And since there was already bomb shelling in the area, we were forced by the Germans to enter the shelters, because we were forced labor workers who were needed for their military effort. I recall that during the Polish uprising, I found a military helmet that I then wore ceaselessly for a few weeks. And so, when I arrived in Germany, my head was almost entirely bald. All of my hair had fallen off, underneath the helmet. Slowly, slowly, during the course of my stay in the forced labor camp, my hair began growing again.

We were three women in the room in this camp. The small portions of food were never sufficient and certainly did not satisfy our hunger. In spite of such dearth, I managed from time to time to save an entire loaf of bread for myself and my two other room-mates. Since I had begun reading at a very early age, I remembered Mark Twain's story about the Chinese man who worked for an employer and wanted a piece of land for himself. He approached the landlord and asked for a plot that he could cultivate. The landlord told him that he would give him the plot providing he climbed the highest mountain and succeeded to survive the freezing temperatures at the peak. The poor Chinese man went to a wise person to seek help. The wise person told him that he could not help, but permitted him to gather twigs and light a fire at the bottom of the mountain so that when he would later be sitting high above, he would see its bright light from a distance, and this might help him to fight the cold of the night. The night passed, and the Chinese man, who had done what the sage advised him, managed to survive. When he reached his landlord, the other man called him a fraud and refused to give him the piece of land; you saw the light, and this is how you survived.

The story gave me inspiration about the bread. We received one loaf of bread a day and never touched it, and the thought about the bread awaiting us added strength and helped us to survive the daily hunger. When we decided, we had bread available for us. We split the loaf into three pieces, one for each, and this way I had my own piece of bread to do with as I pleased.

In the camp, I found a novel way to warm myself. I created a warm blanket from menstrual pads. Many of the women in the camp did not have their periods, and the pads that were supplied to us became the fabric of this blanket. I tied them together and attached them to the piece of cloth I used to cover myself. After I had a few warm nights, the woman who was responsible for our block found my blanket and burnt it. Despite the horrific situation we were in, I could not understand this unwarranted malice, and why she insisted on adding to the horror.

The conditions in the camp were harsh in many aspects. I remember the sight of the Polish girls who waited until the Germans had finished having a smoke, and then took the cigarette butts that were left on the floor, and tried to smoke them.

Another recollection from that period refers to stolen clothes. Every Sunday, the workers arranged a performance, with different groups competing for the privilege of performing on that particular day. Stealing clothes was a necessity, because there were not enough dresses for the performers. And thus, clothes that belonged to different workers would vanish and then reappear somewhere else. This would then be accompanied by an exchange of blows, shouts and threats, but no one interfered, and no one approached the management of the factory, for fear of their over-involvement.

Irka, my good friend, worked at the post office in Krakow and sent parcels to me at the camp, containing food and clothes. I was allowed to receive them. I remember receiving a package that included only one shoe. The other shoe arrived a few weeks later.

And thus I eventually had in my possession one of the most valuable things one could imagine—a pair of shoes. Irka's life story at that period was similar to ours, but she was allowed her freedom in Krakow, perhaps because of her Arian looks.

My daily work at the factory included the screwing of mid-size screws into parts of airplanes. We had neither suitable clothes for the task nor gloves. We worked barehanded, and therefore any possible injury would have ended badly. At the end of the working day, I was commanded to sweep the area in which I worked. Every worker was responsible for the territory she worked in. There were no incidents in those days. One shout from the man or women responsible would silence any attempt to oppose. The treatment of us, the Polish women, was far better than that which the Jewish forced work laborers received there.

From Dina's conversation with Ezra:

Dina: The Germans sent me to work. I was in a destitute state at the time. Sick people were examined and denied entry to Germany, and therefore, I almost did not enter the country. For me, this would have been a disaster, because I had nothing to fall back on in Poland. I had no relatives and no place to go. Germany was the only place that could have saved me, because no one there would know that I was Jewish. And besides, I had nowhere to go to find even one ounce of food. There were many Polish women who escaped. You could escape that place; it was not that difficult. When I spoke to people my age, they suggested that I escape with them. However, I had nowhere to go to; I dreamt only of Germany; this was my only hope for survival.

The train that took us from Poland to Germany had been used initially for cattle. I lay, half fainted, in the car, and next to me lay a Pole—a noble and beautiful woman, who told me that as a result of what had happened to her, she almost did not wish to go on living. Her husband had owned a sugar factory before the war, and they had no children. Their Jewish engineer, before he was taken to the camps, wrote her a letter, and told her that he had given her address to his little daughter, so that she and her husband might rescue her, if possible. After a while, a girl who was seven years of age and looked like an angel came to their house. They had dreamt of having a girl like this, and then she came to them like she was sent from heaven—inside this hell. Her sweetness, her intelligence, her wisdom... this was in 1942 or 1943. They took the girl in and raised her. During the period of the Polish uprising, the girl believed that she had to contribute and decided to become one of the post carriers—children, who delivered messages from place to place. The little girl never returned from one of her missions, and this woman did not know what had happened to her, or even if the girl was still alive. As she told me her story, she cried deeply. I asked her why she was telling me her story, and she said that she knew that I would understand it. I never replied because I had trained myself to be always careful and afraid. I had no idea whom I could trust and whom I could not.

I had no shoes; none at all. I had lost mine while running from place to place and received a pair of wooden clogs instead. When we arrived in Breslau, by the hand of fate, we reached a sugar factory. The owner of the factory was an acquaintance of this woman, as a result of mutual business they had conducted before the war. He came to visit, and she told him that I had no shoes. It so happened that his daughter had the same shoe size as mine, and the following morning I found a pair of shoes next to my bed. And she said to me, "He managed to arrange a way for me to return to Poland, would you like to come back with me?" And then I told her. I told her who I was; I gave her my real name so that she would remember it. And if I would not survive, she would know that she had met me and that I had said that there was nothing for me in Poland. I told her that I did not want to put her at risk. She could not return to Warsaw, as there was nothing there for her. She did not have a home. I told her that she had done one of the best possible things for me that anyone could; I was referring to the pair of shoes.

Ezra: When you told her that you were Jewish…

Dina: She said that she had known, and that this was the reason for telling me her story. This pair of shoes caused me a great deal of trouble with the Polish women with whom I stayed. I have told you that many of them escaped. Those who did had chances of getting settled in Poland. Those who did not did not belong to a very high class. There were prostitutes there as well. They accused me of having relations with the Germans, and said that they were the ones who had given me the shoes. This was a rather miserable beginning. Not wishing to have another reason for concern, I returned the shoes to the woman who had given them to me. I explained to her the reason for this, and she understood. I went back to using the clogs, which served me until we arrived at the frozen labor camp in Germany. We were first placed there, 24 girls in a room, and because no one had anything, each stole from the other. And this was the social group. Later, when I came across information about women's jails, I could compare it to this. Because there are people who, somehow, even during stressful times, keep their perspective, and they keep their soul; everything grows, and they grow inside it. And there are those who shrink and become vicious animals. Those who were there with me, they all shrank. So much so, that during the nights, there were severe beatings between the women. I saw that I was not going to survive with these 24 animals. There were two other girls there, whose behavior was similar to mine; I have their photographs with me. We decided to try to move together into a room for three, which was usually reserved for the *kapo*.[29] Each prisoners' barracks had two such rooms, one at each end. However, how would we manage to move into a room for three? My friend, Irka, who worked back in Poland at the post office, used the name Francis in her certificates. I knew her address and wrote a letter, telling her where I was. She also received a letter from my sister. This was how I found out that my sister was alive and in Germany. When I received a letter from my sister, I once more cried for two days because it felt as though the skies had opened…

Irka began to send to me small parcels that contained mainly tobacco, because you could buy things in exchange for tobacco. To start with, I bought the room for three. I went over to this German, who was responsible for the barrack, and said to her, "Here, have some tobacco; give me a room and you'll have more and more of it." We moved into that room, and it was like night and day. Everything changed. We did not obtain more food; we did not enjoy better conditions, but we were three in a room. We built food storage. We would fast for one day, and take all of the bread and put it in a cupboard. We always had some bread in reserve. This reserve warmed our hearts so much, and

---

29 Kapo—a prisoner in a Nazi concentration camp, who was assigned by the SS guards to supervise forced labor or carry out administrative tasks in the camp. The kapo was given privileges in return for supervising work gangs.

so we created a bubble in which 'we were never hungry,' because we knew that if one of us would be hungry, she could always go there and eat. Interestingly, none of us ate the bread, but it was there for us. A very strong friendship of necessity developed between us but, once again, the Jewish subject came up. They did not know that I was Jewish. Their entire manner of expression about Jews, as well as their attitude towards Jews, annoyed me so much, disturbed me so much, that I could never become a real friend to them. Probably, they felt the same in some way.

In the meantime, I became wealthy, because these parcels that Irka sent were something indescribable. I received a coat, and I received a dress, and I received shoes. Due to the fact that my hair had fallen off during my stay in Warsaw, I used a scarf, and walking around with a scarf was usually considered a sign that the Germans had punished the woman or that she was a whore. Suddenly, my hair grew back again, and I could take off my scarf. They were having concerts on Sunday afternoons, because there were also Italian and French who had resisted the Germans. It was mixed, and they wanted to maintain some kind of standard, so they arranged concerts for people who could perform.

Ezra: And all of this is taking place while the war is going on, and the country is being bombarded. Because for me, the concerts somehow do not fall into line with the war…

Dina: But this is to do with the Germans. The Sunday afternoon concerts were meant to raise morale so that people would work more productively. Because your life cannot revolve only around work, especially when there is no food. There was an Italian there, Nino Pasioli, who suddenly saw me and fell in love with me, and sang for me a song he chose especially for me. Later, the fact that he had fallen in love with me gave me a materialistic advantage; because he knew how to find potatoes. This was not important to me personally, because I already had more food than the others; but we collected the potatoes, and would go over to the forced labor camp for Jews, and we would throw potatoes to them over the fence. He spoke German, and we talked to each other in German, but he also taught me Italian, and I learned many words in this language, and he helped me in this way. I told him.

Ezra: And you were not afraid to tell him?

Dina: I was not afraid because I first spoke with him about the subject. I did not tell him that I was Jewish. I told him that there was a camp there and how much the Jews suffered. So he said "Yes, if we could only help them; perhaps we will do something." This is how I came to know that he was the right address. On the other hand, my two roommates found out that I was going over to the Jews in order to help them, and they did not like it at all. To begin with, this was a disadvantage for them, because I took things from the three of us. I did not split equally between us what Irka sent to me. I threw some over to the Jews. Moreover, I feared that they would find out something. They got a lot out of the friendship that we had amongst ourselves in the room, because I received parcels containing oatmeal fried in butter and used to divide it between us. I was afraid all the same that they might harm me, out of their jealousy of the fact that I was giving some to the Jews. Nino Pasioli helped me in this mission, and his behavior was really extraordinary in this respect. It did not matter that my relationship with him was not based on love, which he knew. However, he did help me in this mission.

I was already corresponding with my sister at the time— via Irka—and I knew where she was. The shelling[30] had already begun. Those who have not gone through such an experience would find it difficult to perceive. Suddenly the skies would turn black, as if in a solar eclipse. Thousands of shells would drop down. Interestingly, I was not afraid of the shelling. You understand. I felt that they could not do anything to me; that they could not harm me. This was my feeling. I worked in a factory, and they bombed factories, but I was not scared of the bombings.

One day, the shelling was massive. They had separate shelters for Ostländers[31] and Deutschen[32]; I ran for shelter and never reached the Ostländer's shelter, as the closest one was that of the Deutschen. I began to enter, but I had on my clothes the letter P, which the Poles wore, similar to how the Jews wore a yellow patch. So they said that this was not the place for me and told me to leave; I left and did not have time to reach the Ostländer's shelter, and so I lay under a tree. I said to myself that whatever will be, will be. I put my hands over my head and thought that this was it. This was a massive shelling, and when it was over, I was told that a bomb had fallen precisely on the side of the shelter where they had refused my entry, and everyone hiding there had been killed by the shock wave. So you see, fate somehow has its way with you.

---

30 A bombing campaign, initiated by the British government and carried out between 1940 and 1945, destroyed or devastated 61 German cities. In February 1942, RAF Bomber Command explicitly began to focus its attacks on the enemy's civilian population, shifting from its strategic bombing to the night-time area bombing of cities, which was designed to break enemy morale.

31 Ostländer—easterner, native or resident of the east, a nickname given to the Poles.

32 Deutschen—Germans in Yiddish and in German.

Ezra: What did they manufacture in that factory?

Dina: Parts for mortars and airplanes.

Ezra: At that time, the war had already closed in on them, and they were reaching the stage of total downfall. How were the Germans? What were they talking about? What were they thinking? Were they saying anything?

Dina: This was incredibly strange. You could already see soldiers walking in the streets lifelessly and wounded, externally and internally. However, at work, it was as if nothing had happened; the same order was maintained; the same thing. They operated the factory till the last day before the evacuation, as though nothing else was going on. This is a tremendous power. I could not comprehend how this could actually be happening.

But I will tell you something: I had an old Meister, whose name was Fritz Donstag. He was responsible for a few casting machines, and I worked the night shift from six pm until six am. This is a terrible shift. It continued endlessly, and you were dying to go to sleep, and the shelling went on and you had to run for shelter. And I stood there and fell asleep; stood and fell asleep. Every time he passed by, he gave me a sort of caress so that I wouldn't fall asleep. He himself did not have much to eat, but he always had for me a small sandwich that he pushed towards me, saying nothing. It contained a bit of margarine and a tiny thin slice of sausage that you could see the sky through; still, it was always there. He had no wax paper and therefore wrapped the sandwich with a small towel. I treated the cloth with great respect and gave it back to him clean and tidy every day.

•

After we had been liberated, Hanka and I insisted on finding the Meister's address in Munich, and we brought to his house a wrapped gift that contained chocolate and canned meat ("bully beef")[33] in quantities that could suffice him for an entire year. He said that if he were to weigh what he had given me against this gift, then our gift was a hundred times bigger, and then he started crying. These were days of unbearable famine for the German population.

•

Ezra: But being on the defeated side, were they saying anything about the war? Were they angry?

Dina: I did not manage to hear anything. Only once, when I had fallen asleep, the old Meister came over and said: "the suffering is about to be over." Because they, too, were afraid. They feared their own shadow. It was a regime of terror. It was a regime of terror not just for the Ostländers, but for the Deutschen, too. The fact is that he helped. That he was not one of them. He was already at the age of retirement. They recruited into their army men who were sixty-five years old and adolescents the age of fourteen.

Ezra: What was the date? When did this period of work at the factory take place?

Dina: From the last few months of 1944 until May 1945, when I was liberated.

---

33 Bully-beef— the canned meat that was supplied to the troops.

The Liberation

Ezra: What happened on the day of liberation? Who showed up?

Dina: The Americans showed up, and for a day or two in advance, there were signs of their arrival, because they started to dismantle the whole factory and send us home. We only feared that they would take us somewhere else from there. But most likely they had no more alternatives, because on both frontiers the situation was already not good. When the Americans arrived that morning, I was already so exhausted that I did not know whether to be very glad. With that, it was a sense of utter liberation that would be difficult to imagine.

Ezra: Try to tell every detail, every encounter.

Dina: Together with the sense of liberation there was also a sense of something very ill-favoured, and this whole encounter ended in an ugly way. The Americans arrived, and we came out to the streets and welcomed them with flowers and kisses, as did the Germans. It was no longer possible to tell who was who, and the Germans too were tired of all of this.

And where did they, the Americans, go afterwards? They entered the Ostländers' refugee camps, those of the Poles, the French and the Italians, because this was where they could celebrate. After all, they would not have gone to the Germans. So those who conquered the town and settled in all the German places were the officers. They gave the simple soldiers limited permission to celebrate, and they arrived at the refugee camps. They got drunk, and I told you earlier that there were all sorts of women in the camps, women who did not mind a strong hug given by an American soldier. However, the soldiers did not distinguish between those who were willing and those who were not, so they tried to hug me too, and I did not want in any way that a drunken American soldier would hug me.

And one soldier came over to me and tried. I told him: "Are you crazy? I'm Jewish." I later thought about why I said those words to him; as if this was what could protect me; what does it mean, "I am Jewish"? I am not Polish; I am not like 'that.' And the strange thing was that this soldier was a Jew from Brooklyn. And suddenly he started crying and fell down on his knees and in his drunkenness, began to ask for forgiveness, and this caused him to sober up. He took me to one side and did not know what to do, he asked for my forgiveness, said that he too was Jewish and that he did not know how to ask for my forgiveness and that this was his first meeting with a Jewish woman after an extended period. And I felt that he was trying to make a martyr out of me, while I was only flesh and blood. Only that he shouldn't touch me—that is all I wanted from him.

The following day he came back. He had some kind of a man's suit, which he gave to me as a present, so that I could turn it into a costume for myself; he started telling me what he had seen on the way to us. It was from him that I first learned about the destruction in Germany that had happened on the way—he had seen how whole cities had been wiped out. He also had seen concentration camps, and he showed me photographs. This was the first time I had seen the Jews standing by the fences looking outwards, and only their eyes were burning, in skeletons. And I understood what had happened there, and I understood that I was even lonelier than I had thought.

Ezra: And up until that moment, in spite of your physical proximity to the events, you had no idea that this is what it was like. No one spoke, and you did not hear.

Dina: I knew because I told you that I had helped the Jews who were held in our forced labor camp; that I had thrown them some food, but could not talk with them. I saw their skeletons moving around in pajamas, but I could not actually speak with them. Even approaching them was dangerous. They were forced laborers, because this was not a concentration camp.

Ezra: Despite them being in the near vicinity, you were unaware of the death camps.

Dina: I was unaware of them. They were nowhere near us; because in Germany itself, do not forget, apart from Dachau and Bergen-Belsen, there really weren't any camps. The camps were in Poland, and we were quite far from them. And as the American army drew nearer, the Germans destroyed the camps.

Ezra: Dina, I wish to make a pause here in the chronological recounting and ask you something. Along the way, throughout those years, and according to your story, and to what I hear—both from the story and from your intonation—the personal struggle—yours and your sister's and perhaps another person close by, with your father and brother being somewhere far, and you not knowing anything. Your war is for your survival. From day to day and from moment to moment, the whole struggle is to survive, and you emphasized this point of how to reach the point of survival while keeping your human qualities. And then suddenly, in those moments of liberation, on the very day that you met the

Jewish soldier who first tried to harass you, and then, after you had put him in his place, told you what was happening, and you suddenly found yourself facing what had happened to the Jewish people; as Itzhak Katzenelson wrote in his poem, "The song of the murdered Jewish people."[34] And suddenly it crossed over from a personal issue into the general Jewish issue. Did anything happen at that stage? When did you begin to feel that Dina was part of an event of this nature that no one had ever foretold or known? How were these entry stages from the personal into the general, as you perceived them at those moments? What happened in you, during the creation of this mental tapestry?

Dina: The process of connecting things together was very difficult because you live in hope the entire time. Hope is the only thing you have. It is the light of this far sun that extends to you its warmth; that perhaps you could go on with your life after the war; that after the war, all will be well. And suddenly the war is over, and a greater hole opened wide up without you knowing its size because this fellow could not estimate how many were murdered and how many survived. He saw horrible things on his way, but did not have the statistics, and the statistics were not relevant at that moment anyway.

What was happening to me was that I was still on my own to begin with. I could not even leave with those two girls with whom I had shared quarters, because I had not told them, even at the moment of liberation, that I was Jewish. I had not known what their reaction would be, or perhaps I did know somehow and was not prepared to suffer again this

---

34 "The Song of the Murdered Jewish People" by Itzhak Katzenelson; translated by Noa H. Rosenbloom http://motlc.wiesenthal.com/site/pp.asp?c=ivKVLcMVIsG&b=476157.

hatred, this grudge, this general animosity for having been lied to the entire time; and since I was waiting for my sister, so that we might do something together, I wanted to leave that camp as soon as possible. I did not know where I was headed. I knew that I would not return to Poland under any circumstances. Whatever the future held for me—to Poland I would not go.

Do not forget that I remained with my Polish name. I was still walking around with a double identity. I still could not tell anyone, because I did not have the necessary certificates. I could not even walk over to the American registration office and tell them: "I am not a Krzeczowska; I am a Minzberg." I had no proof. Anyone could have done it. As long as I had no certificate, I could not talk about it. I waited first for my sister, so that we could decide together what to do.

Ezra: Where was she at that time?

Dina: She was staying in an area that had already been occupied by the Americans. I learnt via Irka that she had remained in a certain place in Dresden, and after the Americans liberated the place where she was staying, she didn't wait, but simply drove with the army to reach me as soon as possible. To this day, I have no idea how she did it, but apparently love and willpower were her driving forces, and nothing could withstand her will. She arrived on the following day—let's say that the Americans conquered the place on Wednesday, well, on Thursday she arrived. She came riding in on an American tank. How she did it, I have no idea. So there was this joy of being together again. I told you that I had felt all along like a leaf blowing in the wind, and now suddenly, I had roots to cling to.

The First Days after the Liberation

Dina: Once more, arose the problem of what to do. If we were to leave the camp, we would need to fend for ourselves. Because in the camp, as much as there was nothing, the Americans made sure that we had food. To leave meant needing to rent an apartment and pay for one's daily supplies. We had no clothes; we had nothing. Here again, my Jewish American soldier, the one with the manly suit, came forward, and arranged jobs for us as Polish and German interpreters inside American headquarters. My sister spoke German well, and we both knew English, which helped us a lot.

We rented an apartment and began to work. However, the entire time, nationalities changed: there were Americans, there were English, and there were Russians; meanwhile the government changed, and the Englishmen came, but that did not bother us. Afterwards, the English turned the area over to the Russians. And here we saw an amazing German phenomenon; overnight, all the Germans somehow found red flags, and when the Russians entered, the whole town was decorated in red. The place turned into a red town without anyone having made a single command. This just went to show the Germans' unyielding self-discipline—red it must be. We had no desire to be under yet another regime, and so we moved together with the English to a nearby town that had not been demolished. It was a beautiful town, and we settled in there, waiting to decide what to do next. We had a place to live with a German lady who must have had a husband who had been in the SS—her closets were stuffed with more furs than she could have managed to wear in a lifetime. I once asked her how she came to possess all these furs. She replied by saying that she had no idea;

that each time when her husband had come from Poland, he brought with him a fur and said that they were very cheap, just a few cents each. We asked her if she had ever asked him how they could have been so cheap in Poland and she replied by saying that she had not asked him. It had been easier for her not to ask. We stayed there and worked with the English, while at the same time, we inquired and received all sorts of information, including the fact that an office for Jews had opened up in Munich, and that there we could find out everything regarding registering and finally obtaining certificates.

Ezra: During this period of shifting between the Americans and the English, did you meet any Jews?

Dina: No. You need to understand one point. The Jews were in camps; no one—the Americans, the English or the Russians—allowed them to leave, because they carried diseases. Their conditions were no better than they had been under the Germans, except that more food was undoubtedly supplied, and no one killed them. Regarding accommodation and comfort, however, they stayed in the same conditions, because they were not allowed as yet to wander about. There was such chaos that just a few who had the courage or the ability succeeded to break out. There were also many sick people—so we did not meet Jews.

Ezra: During the whole period, did you have an opportunity to think to yourself, or together with your sister, about what had motivated the Poles who helped you? From the coal merchant Janek, to Stefkova, and to the others? What were your views about those people who risked their lives and perhaps the lives of their families, had they been caught, to help Jews? Did you have a chance to wonder why you were helped, or did the days still leave no room for thought?

Dina: There was no time to stop and think, and yet the whole time it was somewhere in the background. I asked myself why had this fellow been coming with Janek to visit us, so that we were not alone in Stalowa Wola? He came from a mixed family. They were Swedes. His father was Swedish, but they had been born in Poland and received a Polish education. They hid Jews in their home, and once he had offered to hide a Jew with a beard. He was told to at least have the man shave off his beard, because if someone came and saw someone with a beard, it would present an immediate danger. To this he had replied that he was already endangering himself; therefore, why should he cause anguish? "To remove from a Jew his beard is like removing his personality. If I keep him, I want to keep him sane." Those words caused me to believe once again that humanity exists.

If you do not believe in God, you have to believe in something, and the only belief I had was in human beings, and each person who behaved like a human being added life to me, because it gave me something to hang on to. So these grips, these acts of helping me or others, did not represent only help, but also a grip on life. It was another anchor. You cannot say that I did not value it strongly enough because this question related not only to life; it related to the whole of my being, the whole of my belief, the value of survival. If there are people such as these, then it is worthwhile to survive. If such people do not exist, then what is the point of living? This is why I was not surprised by their reason to act this way.

Ezra: You do a favour for someone, but you really endanger your-self, your parents, your children. That person is craving life too. Where does one draw the line? There has to be a line. I do not love the word sanctity, but one has to reach such high human levels within oneself to act in this manner. From that person's standpoint, I would need to ask him: have you gone mad? One Jew more, one Jew less, you have your family. If I were to provoke him, I would say, "You are irresponsible, why do you do this?" That is his or her side.

On your side, how do you view it? Is it obvious that a person needs to behave in such a manner? I do not know how to explain it. This is why I stand to this very day and salute them. The salutation as a symbol. I salute because there are not enough words to comprehend and to estimate the danger. It is not as if you have money, and you give some of it to charity; you give your life; you might lose your life. Do you live with this feeling that these characters perhaps entered into your being? I am trying to think about the dimension it may have entered; because you are actually alive thanks to them. I am just trying to connect to this situ-ation and wonder if you and your sister spoke about it.

Dina: We spoke about it because this was the essence of life. However, I compare it more to a situation of someone drowning in the water; if there are people who can help because they are good swimmers, they do not think, but rather jump into the water, because this is the way of thinking—someone drowns, and you give them a hand. And if you are already in the water, then it becomes sort of a sport, taking a risk; you save another one and another one. There were those who hated the Germans so much for what they were doing that this was their way of inter-fering. However, most of those who helped Jews actually did it because of the feeling of something sacred; I cannot explain it otherwise. Some godly feature inside of them caused them to do it. There were also very few. More than once, I found myself wondering how such a person might be repaid, for what he had done. And I told you that the young man who used to come and visit us really liked me. Janek liked my sister, but the other fellow was really fond of me. I do not even know his family name. He kept it very secret; he worked in the underground and did not want us to know. So he sat next to me and said, "I really want to kiss you, but I will not do it because you might think that my ability to help you gives me some kind of power over you and that you owe me. So, for now, I will not touch you. Perhaps after the war ends, when we meet again, we will be on equal grounds, and then I will make my move." But now, you realize, it reached the stage in which it would be difficult to believe that a person could overcome these things. He said, "I will not touch you as long as I am not sure that you can say no." So if you meet such people, then it is worthwhile to go on living. Because inside this chaos, you can also see the light.

Ezra: Like my mother used to say, "These are the good messengers." Those who are believers tie it in with God and the emissaries. However, sometimes, the messengers set out without receiving God's command, and this is how you felt.

Dina: This is how we felt towards them.

Ezra: And now let us move on. Did you take leave of the owner of the suit?

Dina: Yes. He traveled with the Americans; we stayed with the English in a different place, and we had to decide first who we were—Jews or *goyot* (gentiles)—and where we belonged.

If we wanted to return to being Jewish, we needed to get to Munich, because that was where the center was located.

Ezra: The difficulty in making this decision was only with regard to this period in time, or whether you would be Jewish altogether?

Dina: We had difficulties regarding whether we would change our name and continue to live a lie. Because there were those who did it. They returned to Poland with their Polish names and never changed them back. However, this was no longer part of the agenda, and we decided to go back to the name Minzberg, which meant returning to the Jewish circle. My sister said, "I will remain at work in the meantime. You will go to Munich."

Ezra: Returning to the name Minzberg meant returning to the family circle, to the Judaism from whence you had come. By the way, at this point, did you know anything about your mother or father?

Dina: Nothing. There were no letters. No post at all. No telephones. Germany was in ruins. The trains served only the American army. There was no possibility of purchasing a ticket and traveling to Munich.

Ezra: You maintained contact with your mother and father up until a certain point, and the assumption was that they were still alive.

Dina: We were not thinking about this yet. It had not come to this stage. We now wanted to start something new. It was so difficult. You feel that you are up in the air and have no idea what's going on with you. I was twenty-one, a young woman, and I was gaunt because there was so little to eat after the war. I had no clothes, but somehow, slowly, we managed in that area as well, and I traveled to Munich dressed in the uniform of a Polish soldier in the British army. I do not wish to go now into all the hardships that accompanied my journey. I was by myself. My sister stayed behind to keep our jobs. I traveled and found myself in a godforsaken station. There were no trains, and there was nothing there. The soldiers dropped me at one particular station and told me that this was as far as they could take me, and that from that point on I was to travel on my own.

A very long train arrived, and black American soldiers disembarked. This was the first time I had seen black people, except maybe in a photograph. I approached the commanding officer; I always approached the commanding officers, since they were older, more responsible and more educated. I briefly told the officer my story, and he said, "You are our guest." They took me to their carriage, where they placed a folding bed for me and a guard who sat next to me. As I was falling asleep, I heard them comparing the colours of our hands. I arrived at the station before Munich, and this officer handed me over to an English officer, saying, "Take this lady and bring her to Munich." The British officer looked at him and said: "Lady?" in a mocking manner, as if someone who travels in the black people's carriage is no longer a lady. I traveled with the British, and the British officer had some sort of a German woman inside one of the carriages, and he came out from there sweating each time and also tried to make a pass at me. I was never so angry at someone the way I was angry at him, and I told him he should go back to the black soldier and learn some manners from him. "You take advantage of my weakness now, after everything I went through." He was so ashamed that he did not know what to do with himself, and because of his feelings of shame he gave me all of his battle rations and chocolate. I told him that this would not compensate me and that I did not even have the strength to carry it. "Take it and share it," I said.

Sometimes we get to see all of the stigmas. All of a sudden, I saw that human beings are bad and degenerate, wishing to take advantage of one another – all kinds of things that one would have thought would vanish after the war, leaving everything bright and beautiful. However, people do not change so much.

In Munich, and by sheer accident, I met Pocicz, my cousin's husband. He had been liberated from a camp and was organizing a Jewish committee in Munich. There were hardly any Jews in Munich, and lists of those who survived began to arrive. The primary task of the committee was to collect as many names as it could, so that people could find their relatives. I wrote a letter to my sister telling her that she could come. Once we were together again, we began to work as part of the Jewish committee, in the department for tracing relatives.

•

In Munich, we found accommodations with a German family. The apartment was given to us by the Germans themselves, and we settled there. We discovered that in the early days of the war, the family, which was registered with the Nazi party, had allowed their daughter to marry a Jewish man. The couple had gone to America and left behind them an empty apartment. Most likely, someone wanted to pay the family back for betraying the Führer, and gave their address as a permanent place of residence for any needy person, and this is how we arrived at the apartment.

The apartment was equipped with a kitchen and utensils, an oven and a heater, and beds that allowed a good night's sleep. This was an excellent sleep for two women who had not seen an ordinary bed for a few years by then.

•

Dina:　And there is still no contact with my mother, my father or my brother. There are no letters; there is nothing. There is no possibility of traveling to Poland. The country is in chaos; there are Russians there—and we fear the Russians and do not want to go there, as the Russians had conquered Poland.

Once, we were traveling on a public train, and I heard two Jews talking to one another. One says, "If it were not for Minzberg, I would not be alive." That only goes to show how small a place the world is. We hear these words, and I go over to him and say, "Pardon me, who is the Minzberg you were talking about?" and he answers, "Marek Minzberg." "And what did he do for you?" "He gave me money and clothes and fed me. If it were not for him, I would not be alive." "So please give me his address, because I happen to be his sister." This was a very emotional encounter—to receive, in such a manner, news about our brother; that he was in Tashkent,[35] that he was doing well and that he was there together with our father and some cousins of ours. Later, they were to leave Tashkent as soon as they could. Some time passed, and we found out that my brother and my father had already arrived in Krakow. There was no way to communicate at that point. Slowly, slowly Jews started coming to Germany from all over, probably because

---

35 Tashkent—capital city of Uzbekistan (formerly the USSR).

Germany served as a place of reunion. No one could depart from Poland to Palestine or anywhere else. My sister and I faced a dilemma. My mother arrived in Munich first. She knew that we were already there. She came to our place and lived with us, and never stopped talking about America.

Ezra: How old was your mother at that time?

Dina: Fifty-eight. And she started talking about America, and America, and America since this had been embedded in her even from before, and she hated everything Polish. She would not go back to Poland. She would only go to America. In the meantime, I met in Munich all kinds of Israeli elements, and encountered, in the Jewish Committee, a young man from Czechoslovakia, who was a very enthusiastic Zionist.

Ezra: Was this the first time you met an Israeli person?

Dina: Yes. Yes.

Ezra: Apart from the guide who had once been in Israel?

Dina: Yes.

Ezra: How was this meeting for you?

Dina: To me, they were demi-gods. Surely, they were modest, and as much as they could, they offered encouragement. They brought with them more books than food or money. They brought photographs of the land. It was more a matter of spiritual content with them. Because most anyone who saw a poor Jewish woman after the war gave her something to eat. So we did not lack food; rather books and those sorts of things—symbols—were missing. He had this dry olive leaf that he carried with him everywhere. And he gave me this leaf, which was very precious to me. And something began to grow in me in an extraordinary way. I probably had an inclination towards it, because I told my sister that I would not go to America, not to Poland, and I most certainly would not stay in Germany. I started to cook up a rebellion against my parents, because if we did not travel to America then perhaps they would not either.

Ezra: And this was a rebellion against your sister as well, or were you in agreement?

Dina: We were of the same mind and the same body, because we were like... you know, when we slept, even if we had two beds, we always slept together and turned over as one body. There was some kind of understanding between us, some sort of love; she was willing to sacrifice everything for me. She was much more mature than me, also from the mental standpoint. As I said earlier, in 1938, she read Hitler's *Mein Kampf*, and she said that she believed everything he said. "A man who is a lunatic needs to be in a mental hospital, but he is not in a mental hospital, he is the ruler, and therefore I believe every word he says." Anyhow, I learnt from her one thing—when you want to become acquainted with something, read about it, and judge for yourself without asking anyone else. Your common sense should tell you if it is true or not.

Ezra: So, you have no argument with your sister. Both of you, as you said, were of one mind and turned around together. This turning around is given as an analogy.

Circles

Dina: What were also vital for me were circles. I want to explain what I mean by circles. I had not had any circles since leaving home. The family circle had been broken. I had been alone. This loneliness is a most terrible thing that, until you've experienced it, you have no way of understanding. You are alone from the family standpoint, from the national standpoint, and even from the standpoint of your own views. There is no circle; there is nothing that connects you with anything else. You try in all sorts of ways. There is no circle. You can join a line, but you cannot participate in a circle. When you are ejected from a circle, you are thrown out. I wanted to return to any kind of circle, and when I arrived at the Zionist movement in Munich, people were dancing in circles. This dancing in circles has in it a magic that is much greater than what it appears to be—it is not just a circle; it is an unbreakable chain; this is something very powerful and very important to someone who has no roots in the land; yet this chain supports them.

Ezra: This feeling that you are describing now—is it what you felt when you saw the circle of dancers and wanted to join it?

Dina: Yes. That it was something that could hold me.

Ezra: So, you break into the circle.

Dina: Yes. I break into and join the circle.

Ezra: And your sister who turns around together with you, does she break and join with you?

Dina: Not to the same extent.

Ezra: She is older.

Dina: She is older and holds responsibility in relation to our parents. She allows me. She always allows me to be less responsible. She knows that my brother is with Father, and that Mother is here, and she waits for my father and my brother to arrive, so that a decision can be made together. She says to me, "You will go in the meantime. You will be the spearhead. If you are there, we will all come. We need to establish some sort of a colony in Palestine."

Ezra: It was still Palestine?

Dina: *Eretz Yisrael.*

Ezra: For your mother this is perhaps still Palestine and America. For you, it is *Eretz Yisrael* with this olive leaf, the photographs, and the circle. So you go to *Eretz Yisrael*. How was this woven and changed from words into action? Did you agree with the fact that you were going? Did you decide to take leave?

Dina: I agreed because I knew that the separation would be short and that my sister would follow me. Even if our parents would not do so, she would still follow me.

Ezra: You knew it or did she promise you?

Dina: She said, "You will leave, and I shall follow." I later received all sorts of letters from her, and she wrote to me in one of them, "You see how my eyes are sad because I am not with you." And she also said something like, "If father will come here, and Marek will come here, we will not be able to untangle it so quickly; they will not let you go; so you must go now." And she probably did not have to convince me too much because I was ready and prepared to go to Israel; I wanted to obtain a new identity as soon as possible.

I had in me something that I cannot explain, and perhaps not everyone had the same experience.

Ezra: But a person can obtain a new identity also in America, even though this may not have been easy.

Dina: While working in Munich after the war, different people approached me. A young man came along, and his name was Polack. The Polack family had been completely Polish prior to the war. He had not known then that he was Jewish. They were called Polack, and his appearance was entirely Polish, and all of a sudden they informed his father that he had to go to a camp. He had actually been captured. Otherwise, he would have escaped. He was in a Jewish hell without feeling Jewish. And he told me, this was practically a joke. "This was real irony," he said, "because I did not want to be Jewish and they forced me to be Jewish, and the whole time I was not even inside the circle of Jews. What did they want from me?" And then he says to me, "I have an older brother who was married to a girl. They became Jewish in the full sense of the word, and now they want to go to Palestine, but I want to go to America and obtain a new identity. My family name is Polack, but I do not want to be a Jew. However, if I go to America, I will not have a brother, because he will be in a different place altogether and will feel differently, and I will be, once again, alone. If I go to Palestine, I will feel as a foreign element there. What will I do there?" Through him, I understood all of my doubts, and how it was for me. His doubts permitted me to see the picture of what would happen if I went to America and became once again… what? What would I become there?

Anyhow, we decided that I would go. I contacted this friend who worked with the "Bricha,"[36] and they gave me a date for departure with the group.

---

36 Bricha (escape)—This was the name of a Zionist para-military organization that planned and carried out the Illegal transfer of European Holocaust survivors to Mediterranean ports of embarkation for Palestine.

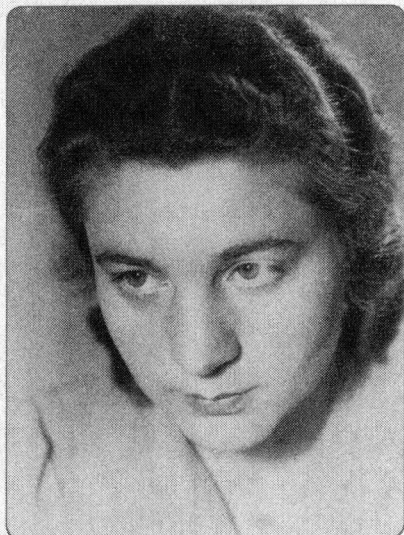

Hanka, my sister, Koszyce, 1942

In Koszyce, 1942

With Irka, my friend, 1942

With Hanka, my sister,
Koszyce, 1942

With Bishe and Irka,
my friends, 1942

With Irka, my friend, Koszyce, 1942

Janek Mlynarczyk

Janek and his wife after the war

With Hanka, Gutman, Weingarten and Asher the boy, Koszyce, 1942

My mother, Tonia, Pocicz, my sister, Hanka and
my cousin, Hadassah, in the family home in Koszyce

In Stalowa Wola

With my sister, Hanka,
Stalowa Wola

Zosia Stefkova (In a photograph from 1987)

With Hanka, my sister, Warsaw, 1943

The photograph in my second Arian certificate, which carried the name Genowefa Lubowidzka

Vazik, the boy with whom I worked in "the birdcage" near Warsaw, 1944

In Warsaw during the war, 1944

Marszalkowska Street, Warsaw, during the war

A barricade of Polish rebels during the Polish Uprising
in Marszalkowska Street in Warsaw, August 1944*

[123]

After the war, 1945

With Hanka, my sister, after the war, 15 July, 1945

The route of escape from Koszyce to Warsaw

In Warsaw

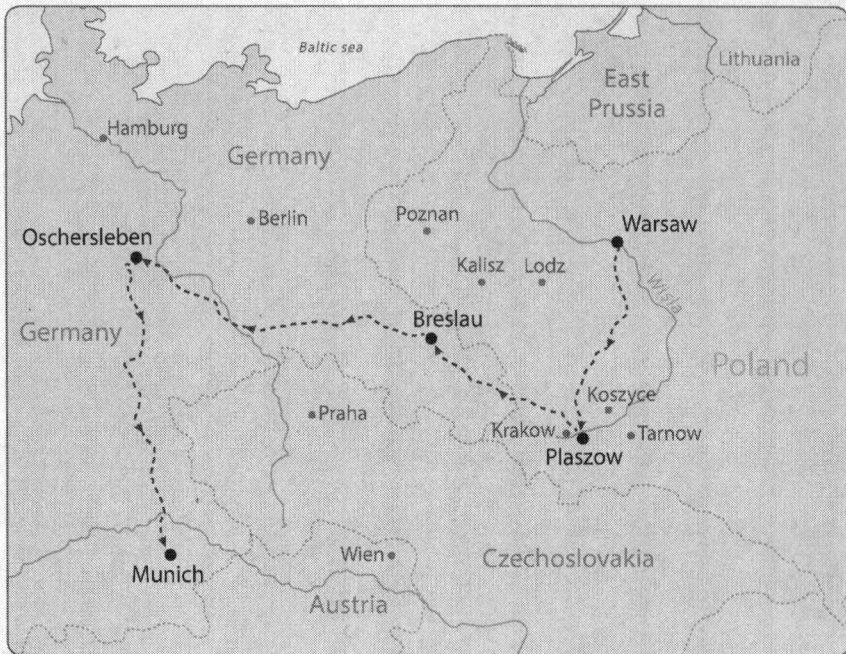

The journey from Warsaw to Germany

Chapter Three

The Journey to Israel

The Transit Camp, Magenta in Italy and the Meeting with Bezalel

From Dina's conversation with Ezra:

Dina: We were departing.

Ezra: Who are "we"?

Dina: A group of people I did not know at all. We departed. I took my bag and left. The young man who had arranged everything did not leave; he stayed. We were on the road—a group of fifty or perhaps sixty people.

Ezra: What was the group's composition? Young people? Adults? Children?

Dina: Most were young people with no families. Because still, you know, I departed rather early.

Ezra: When did you leave?

Dina: At the end of 1945. However, I want to say something beforehand.

Ezra: This was about a year after the war was over.

Dina: The war ended in May 1945. Anyhow, I must emphasize that I do not know how others felt, but I would walk down the street in Munich and feel that every person I met was a Nazi who could have been positioned in a camp or killed Jews. I could not free myself from that thought, not even for a moment, and it accompanied me the entire time.

Ezra: Did this cause you to continue to feel afraid or did it make you think, "Here we are; we have beaten you"? Or did you feel hatred?

Dina: It poisoned my life. It caused an internal poisoning that I could not live with. I think that I left before the end of 1945 because at the end of 1946 I was already on my way to Israel. So we were on our way, and there was a total lack of order. We sat in a truck with our bags on us. It was so unorganized; people were so uncivilized and shouted the whole time; the feeling that all those who had left the camps were only half human was still around. And this was the truth, because they pushed, and they did not trust you, and they always wanted to be first in everything. And there is no wonder about it. Most of them were men. At a certain point, I told them that we had to get out of the truck, arrange our bags and sit on them, and that in this way we would have more room, we would have something to sit on, and it would be more comfortable. And they said to me, "You are really a know-it-all woman; show us; get out of the truck and set an example; perhaps you want us to get out of the truck, and you will not allow us back." But who was I? How could I not allow them back? They had a fear of receiving an order from a higher authority that would prevent them from embarking. I got out, and the driver suddenly started to drive, and I fell out of the vehicle and received a massive blow on my leg, which I did not register so much at that moment. We reached the Austrian border; the crossing was rather smooth; we walked a bit; we managed all right. Finally, we arrived in Milan.

Ezra: After the war, someone described to me that Europe was flooded with people, a migration of entire nations.

Dina: They traveled mainly by train. Trains were traveling with French, Italians, Poles. It was not so easy because most places had been bombed and everything was ruined. The Germans had brought so many people to Germany, and then there was the need to send them back.

I arrived in Milan, and they sent us to camp Magenta[37] near Milan. After a few days, my leg swelled up like a balloon, and they sent me to a hospital in Milan. I underwent surgery and stayed in the hospital for six weeks. It was a large room with forty-eight people in it; all of them lying there together. And I lay in a place where many people came to visit. On a Sunday for example, the beds were blackened because of the many visitors who stood around them. Only I was a lonely island; no one came to visit me. Once again, there was this terrible loneliness.

There was a Shlomo from "HeHalutz"[38] in Milan who visited me, though I wished that he would not, because I did not want to establish relationships with people who were not my relatives; I did not wish to owe anything to anyone. There was a priest who came to visit, and he saw that my bed was lonely, and so he started to visit me, probably hoping to convert me to Christianity. In the meantime, he taught

---

37 For further reading about Magenta camp—please see the appendix page entitled, "The Magenta Immigrants' Camp, Italy."

38 HeHalutz (lit. The Pioneer) was a Jewish youth movement that prepared young people for settling in the Land of Israel. It became an umbrella organization of the pioneering Zionist youth movements.

me Italian, and after six weeks I spoke the language a bit. The nurses were nuns, and on the first opportunity I was allowed to bathe, I went to the shower and washed. One nun came and nearly fainted. I was naked. So she says to me, "This is not how you shower." "So how do I shower?" I ask, and she says, "On the inside; you wear a gown and clean on the inside." So I tell her that if God had created me and was not ashamed, then he would not be ashamed to look at me. She stared at me, and could not comprehend how a person could speak in such a manner about God. I left the hospital and returned to Magenta, and I arrived at my meeting with the Israelis. The Israelis managed Magenta.

Ezra: You had already met Israelis in Munich.

Dina: In Munich, I met Israelis who were born in Poland or Germany, and probably, most of the Brigade[39] soldiers were not born in Israel. In Magenta, I met Israelis. One evening, I recall, two guys arrived. They were not tall, but it could be that I perceived them to be much taller. One of them was Zorik, Dalia's brother. The other one lives now near Tel Aviv. I saw him recently at a concert, and I suddenly realized how short he is, but back then he seemed much taller to me. They wore shirts with horizontal stripes—sailors' shirts. They were tanned and unshaven. They looked like people from another planet. I did not understand a word in Hebrew.

There was one character there; they called him Churchill, and he had brought with him from Israel his accordion, and

---

39 The Jewish Infantry Brigade Group was a military formation of the British Army composed of volunteers from the Jews in Mandatory Palestine. The Brigade served in Europe during World War II and its soldiers fought the Germans in Italy. After the war, some of them assisted Holocaust survivors to emigrate illegally to Mandatory Palestine.

he taught us how to sing Israeli songs. He was such a fine man, full of strength. He had also brought with him records and arranged a concert for us. Every afternoon, those who wished could listen. However, there was one thing he asked—complete silence. This desire to educate, to give. We felt so distant from it. They were not big talkers. They did not speak English. There was hardly any communication with them. Most of them did not speak Yiddish, and I did not speak it too well either. There was not a language I could use in order to communicate with them.

Ezra: With the kind of home you came from, you did not know Yiddish?

Dina: During the war, I made an effort not to know Yiddish because that would have caused all kinds of words to enter my language.

Ezra: But at home, you did speak Yiddish.

Dina: Yes, but not with the housekeepers, and most of the conversations were with the housekeepers.

Ezra: Let us return to the camp.

Dina: The camp was organized in such a way that we were actually independent. We used to cook and wash our laundry by ourselves. There were different groups there, and I was assigned to the Czech-Hungarian group that later went to Kibbutz Hamadia. I had no idea what was happening politically in Israel and had no idea to which group I should belong. Gordonia was there, so I joined Gordonia. I told you that I had to be associated with a circle. We lived together, three girls. In the beginning, I did not know that this was also the camp where the Hagana's[40] ammunition, fuel and food were kept. They also had there a small workshop that was used for preparing bunks for the ships. This was the preparation camp for the ships of the *Ma'apilim*.[41]

Ezra: Apart from organizing concerts, singing songs and joining a circle, did anyone prepare you? Did anyone act as translator between you and those who did not speak your language? What was the feeling after all the moving around? Did this last change sit well with you?

Dina: Yes, I began to feel it. We rose early in the morning with the sports coaches. One of them was Bezalel. It was freezing outside. They seemed to always be warm because they were the coaches. They used to line us up in a row, all of *di paddles*[42] of yesterday and train us in gymnastic exercises and running—very much like the beginning of a small army. Later, there was a lecture and a Hebrew lesson. Then we washed our laundry. The days were organized. We cooked in turns. We were not idle. There was a medical clinic there. There was a classroom. Everyone had to be in some sort of defined activity. And the whole time, Israelis would come and Israelis would go. Because this was some kind of a meeting point; they would send them from there on to France, to open another camp. Each of these camps had an Israeli who was in charge. And of these, Yehuda Harari had the brains to see things for what they were, and he arranged for as many of the refugees as possible to become partners in the work; besides, there were not enough Israelis

---

40 Haganah (lit. The Defense) was a Jewish paramilitary organization in the British Mandate of Palestine (1921–48); it became the core of the Israel Defense Forces (IDF).

41 Ma'apilim—Illegal Jewish immigrants during the British mandate period.

42 di paddles—Yiddish, meaning carcasses, slouches.

to bring over for this purpose. So they appointed someone in charge of the food; someone else to be in charge of the sewing workshop; and a third person to be responsible for the ammunition. All sorts of things started to become organized from within the place, and this is how I met Bezalel. He was in transit from Israel to Marseille.

Ezra: This is where you actually meet the remains of the Jewish people, who had been put into ruins. So, apart from the dancing and exercises and everything else you may have been doing, you heard Jews telling their story? Or was it a case of each one to him or herself?

Dina: Everyone wanted to talk. Everyone wished to tell the others what he or she had gone through.

Ezra: What happened then, in the camp, when people met, and stories met; when all kinds of stories gathered together in one place? How did you feel? Because you had no idea what the concentration camps had been like, and there, in this camp, there were already people who had arrived from the concentration camps. Did you witness the Israelis as listeners? Describe to me the experience of meeting with the remains of the Jewish people.

Dina: This was an incredibly painful meeting because, to begin with, you are still filled with your own pain, and you lick your own wounds, and this usually takes much longer than you might think. When you begin to feel more comfortable, to feel better and more secure, then you are free to deal with all of your own pain. You hear people, and you become filled up very quickly, and you do not wish to hear anymore because it is so horrible, so horrific and it repeats itself. The stories are similar. And you want to shut yourself up somehow and not get to know so much, because the more you know, the more it hurts.

You do not even know how to contain all of this pain; you are still hurting; you are still not settled with everything you have gone through. And thus, those who had survived were not interested in telling the others who had also survived, because it did not make much of an impression on them. A person who has experienced extreme pain cannot share the pain of someone else. You must be somewhat vacant and free of pain to absorb the pain of someone else. Otherwise, it repeatedly bounces off the wall.

So, they found the appropriate victims for their stories—the Israelis. And I heard from Bezalel that he could not talk about it for years; that he could not hear about it. He was furious; to begin with, he was outraged. If someone came and told him how he had been persecuted and forced, he was infuriated at how this person had allowed, at how he had permitted, for something like this to be done to him. He was also furious at those who had done it, but his anger was more towards the Jews, the burning insult of the Jews. Each Israeli was offended at being a partner to the extreme insult to the Jews; to the fact of turning human beings into beasts; to the fact that the purpose was humiliation. They could understand death better than humiliation. And this caused extreme pain, and indeed produced something internally, and I do not believe that any of the Israelis who met the Holocaust survivors in Europe came back to Israel the same.

So, to begin with, this meeting was a horrible shock, as a result of the event, which later became a kind of indifference. You could not hear, and you did not want to listen.

You reached the limits of pain, and it could reach this far and no further. And because I am in the process of telling you things now, I felt yesterday rather exhausted. Because I think that this is the first time I have sat and talked about these things, the reason being that I do not wish to hear any more about it, and because Bezalel did not want to hear, I did not tell much about it at home. It was some kind of an agreed to silence that I will not cause him pain, and that I will educate the children without it.

Ezra: I have to digest what you are telling me, but let us go back to the camp, and only later we will talk about the other times with Bezalel. At this time, Bezalel was a guide in the camp.

Dina: He was not there yet. He had visited only for one day.

Ezra: If he was not there, then who was? Do you know if this was the *Palyam*,[43] or were these fellows from the British logistics corps?

Dina: But they were not guides. First came Avraham Zakai; later there was someone called Fabia, who had been born in Germany; then came someone named Peter, whose head was bold and who seemed older; then there was Churchill and Moshe Rabinowitz and Ossi Ravid. There were big Uzi and small Uzi. Most of these names were not the real names, which made it impossible to track these people later on. Each of them managed the camp for a time and prepared the people for their immigration.

Ezra: Did you leave the camp and mix with the Italian community?

---

43 *Palyam* (an abbreviation of Plugat HaYam, lit. Sea Company) was the naval unit of the Palmach (the elite fighting force of the Haganah in the years 1941-1948). The *Palyam* became the core of the Israeli Navy Seals later on, called Shayetet 13.

Dina: Not with the community. We would go to the movies and out on trips, but we were careful not to mix with the locals, because the camp had a larger number of people fictionally registered than their actual number, in order to receive more bread and more sugar and to collect more food for the ships. So when they used to come to visit, when the police came to count us, we would put on a show—we would run around the camp and change our clothes, and be counted again. And they could not tell, because all of the Jews looked alike, and by comparison, we actually did not look too well, but we would disguise ourselves and dress up, and they would count, and so instead of 100 people, they counted 500. Meanwhile, the Italians watched and knew what was happening, and yet they probably had enough sense of guilt, which caused them to help us, because, after all, they had not spared us from suffering.

Ezra: There was this kind of Italians, and there were others.

Dina: But their regime had been against us, and they felt that they had not offered enough help. I have no reason to be angry with the Italians, on the contrary. At times, I had to go to Magenta. We stayed in a villa outside the village. The villa was called Villa Fasano, and the headquarters were there. We would not allow people in there so easily, because of the ammunition and the fuel. Later, I became in charge of the food storage. When they wanted to scare me, they would tell me—Dina, the storage is on fire. After some time, I stopped believing them, until one day the storage was really burning, and I did not go. It burnt because it contained American matches, and there were also mice, and probably a mouse passed through and somehow lit a match and everything caught fire. Coffee that was stored in big boxes exploded, and we lost a significant amount of food. That was a massive damage.

Ezra: When did they tell you that soon you were to board the ship? When did the term "*Ma'apilim* boat" appear? When did all that was going on become clear to you?

Dina: Instantly. When I arrived at the camp, one group had already left to rendezvous with the ship. We knew exactly where we were heading. We knew how many of us should be on the ship. We were partners to the preparations.

I want to tell you how Bezalel arrived at the camp. One evening a few fellows came, and in their honour, we arranged beds in a special room. Our camp was some kind of a transit camp, and people would come for a while, and then travel from there to wherever they were meant to go. We were three in a room—Bluma, Hennia and I—and we are still in touch with each other. This room was very pleasant; we had a radio, and we used to invite people over to sit and have coffee. We had a good stove, and the room was warm. It is cold in Milan during the winter. So they came, the fellows who were already there, and together with them came another fellow, and we sat on some kind of a sofa. We sat at a distance from each other, not next to each other. Someone started singing, someone started talking, and Bezalel stretched his hand behind someone's back, and our hands met without us knowing whose hand we were touching. I did not extend my hand in order to meet his, but there was so much warmth in him and so much spark that I looked at him, and he looked at me, and we did not break the hold of our hands.

Ezra: Does he also agree that this happened by accident?

Dina: He says that perhaps this was on purpose, maybe not; he could not remember. Later on, we arranged a bed for them, and in the morning, they disappeared. I knew which was the bed he had slept in. His bed was the most organized one. Today I know that he is not organized at all, but, back then, I really liked the fact that his bed was so organized and neat. He went without leaving me a note. Nothing. He went to Marseille, took a ship from there and returned after three or four months. When he arrived, it was once more together with many fellows.

Yehuda Arazi—the person in charge—was supposed to come and decorate them with medals. I recall that someone said that Arazi had arrived, but the camp's gate was locked. Bezalel gave me his hand, and we ran together to open the gate. When we returned, he said to me in English, "I do not think that I will accept this medal. He has no right to give medals, and I also do not wish to have one. I do not work for decorations." This was something so noble; I do not know how to explain it to you. Arazi arrived; there were lovely refreshments, and we danced and sang, and then suddenly Arazi says that he wishes to give out the medals. The fellows stood up and stated that they would not accept them. I remember how this was something that accompanied me the entire time and played over and over in my head—the fact that they would not accept the medals. I really liked it. I cannot explain to you; it was so different from the army, where you decorate with a medal and salute; and here, people do things in order to do them and not for nonsense. Bezalel became responsible for the camp; we were already practically a couple, and once we traveled in some kind of...

Ezra: How old was he?

Dina: He was twenty-two years old. He is one year older than me.

Ezra: He was twenty-two years old; he arrived with the *Palyam*, and he was in charge of the camp.

Dina: Let me go back a bit in the story: We used to go to the movies. We always travelled using this kind of wheeled platform. One time we were on our way back, singing, and he said to me, "Comrade you are off-key," which hurt me very much. And if I was off-key, so what? He did not even know my name, even though he had given me his hand and we had run together to the gate.

All sorts of people, representatives of UNRWA[44] and The Joint,[45] who came from Germany to Italy on their vacations, used to come and see me, because I was the one who had been in Munich. And the *shlichim*[46] saw that men in uniforms from UNRWA and representatives of The Joint came to visit me, and they did not like it at all. And they thought, perhaps she is a spy after all. She speaks English; she has visitors from all sorts of armies. The matter has to be investigated, and a responsible action must be taken, because there is ammunition here. They probably

---

44 UNRWA: United Nations Relief and Works Agency for Palestine refugees in the Near East.

45 Joint or JDC—American Jewish Joint Distribution Committee—a Jewish relief organization based in New York City. The JDC was founded in 1914, initially to provide assistance to Jews living in Palestine under Turkish rule.

46 Shlichim—emissaries who represent Jewish-Zionist organizations and work with Jews in the Diaspora.

consulted with Arazi, and he told them, "Send her over to me and I will look into the matter."

He said that he would check it by saying that he needed help in his house, because the woman who had held this position had traveled to Israel, and he needed someone else to run his house. He lived by himself. And truly, there was always someone in the house who answered the telephone. They bring me to him, saying that he wants to speak to me regarding a job in his house. He spoke excellent Polish. He was charming. He was older than the other fellows by a few years, and they, therefore, called him "The Old Man." He had a slight limp in one foot; he had probably been injured by something. So he starts to explain to me about the job, and so on, and later he asks me where I come from. I tell him that I am from Poland, and he asks what my family name is, and I reply, Minzberg. He then goes on to say that he knows a Minzberg from Lodz. I respond and say that I do have an uncle who used to be a *shaliach* in Lodz on behalf of *Agudat Yisrael*. He then tells me that his cousin is married to one of my cousins. So, we are already related. He did not tell me the truth, and only years later did I learn about the reason for that interview. He told me a beautiful story in Polish. Later I entered his study, and on the desk, I saw a photograph of a man of Russian origin. There was something lovely about this man. I ask him, "Who is this?" And he says, "This is Eliyahu Golomb." He made it sound as if the name was as important as that of Herzl, and so I did not dare to ask who Eliyahu Golomb was, lest I be seen as ignorant. I told him that I did not intend to stay with him and that I was travelling back to Magenta. He said that if this was the case, and we were related, then I would be given responsibility over the food. So this relationship cost me another year in Italy.

Ezra: So, is this a year of work or did you feel a deeper sense of mission, in which you were here to help others? What is the feeling that accompanied you throughout the year?

Dina: It had two aspects. First of all, I knew that this was a duty; that someone had to do it; that there were not enough people who came from Israel, and that those they did send would usually be trained to carry out a particular duty. And do not forget that I had Bezalel there. I wanted to be near him, and that was a vital point, because as I already told you, the way I was, the feeling I had of being outside the circle; when I met Bezalel, it was as if I had suddenly found my other half. And this may sound very romantic or not so realistic, but it is realistic because I felt this way, and it has proven itself, and stood the test of time. So, for me, this was not a waste of time, because it had already started to be my future.

•

Bezalel was love at first sight for me. In my eyes, he had a great deal of integrity and qualities that one cannot find in every human being. He pursued justice and law. He reminded me of the judges from the Bible. When I met him, I wanted to tell him, "Where have you been this whole time; I was searching for you… I have found my soul mate."

And this is how Bezalel told it in his book:[47]

"The Spy"

When Dina Minzberg arrived at the Magenta camp, she stood out with her beauty, her self-confidence and her command of the English language, something that was unusual with the Ma'apilim.

It can be said now that I fell in love with her at first sight, and that I had hoped the feeling would be mutual. There was one thing that bothered me very much. Every now and then, UNRWA and Joint officers, with whom she had worked back in Germany, came to visit her. Since our activities in Magenta were clandestine, I feared that amongst those visitors were British spies who might have uncovered the underground activities taking place in the camp. After quite a few hesitations, I approached Yehuda Arazi and told him of my concern that Dina Minzberg was a British spy.

Arazi responded to my words in a solemn manner and invited Dina to his office in Milan. After a thorough investigation in Polish, Arazi found out not only that Dina was not a spy, but that she was a family relative of his. He offered her a job in his office in Milan, but Dina refused because her heart was in Magenta. And this is how "the spy" returned to me and has never left my side to this very day.

When Arazi and Edna Sereni found out about the growing romance between Dina and me, they did not welcome the relationship. The two probably feared that I would bestow upon Dina extra privileges; and that this would enrage the other immigrants and bring about tension on the ship. For this reason, they instructed me to move to the ship Arlozorov. To my delight, after a while, and for technical reasons, I was taken off the ship and sent back to the camp. "And this time, in order to make sure that they would not separate us again, he discriminated against me, so that heaven forbid, no one would claim to the contrary," tells Dina later on.

•

---

47 Page 67 in Bezalel Drori's book, *BeGalim SoArim* (Upon Stormy Waves), which tells his life story (published in 1999).

Ezra: And what about your sister and your mother?

Dina: They were all still in Germany.

Ezra: When do you write to your sister for the first time about having a boyfriend? When do you let her in on the secret?

Dina: First, I write to my parents, telling them that I want to come to Germany with my boyfriend so that they can meet him, because I didn't know what to write about him, for what could I write? That he is a fisherman? That he is in the *Palyam*? They were not familiar with those terms; they did not know what they meant. He had told me that he was a member of Kibbutz Hulata and that he was a fisherman. Those were his prospects in life. I could not impress my parents with these, so I wrote to them that he was a great Zionist. I do not know if this made an impression on them. I could not write to them that he was a scholar, that he was religious, that he was a doctor or anything else; none of these were relevant. So, the first thing I wrote to them was that he was a great Zionist and that this should suffice. And he allowed himself to laugh and said that he would enter and say some sort of a Beduin sentence in order to embarrass me; that he will introduce himself as he was. Anyhow, it did not come to this, because, in the midst of our preparations for the visit, it was decided that Bezalel was to lead a ship.

Ezra: Was there a stage at which you were angry with your parents for not joining you on the way to Israel?

Dina: No, no.

Ezra: Did you feel good being on your own?

Dina: I did not think along this line at all.

Ezra: And what about your sister?

Dina: My sister, with her I knew things would be alright. She led a very interesting life. She worked over there and met interesting people. I received regards from her as well as letters. The rest of the family had arrived in Munich, and Father received a job on The Jewish Committee, and my brother got settled. I was not worried about them. I knew that if I went to Israel, they would all follow me.

Ezra: When you say that your brother got settled, what was he doing there?

Dina: He was buying and selling like everyone else. He had not spent any time in a camp. He came to Germany, directly to Munich, and there he had an apartment. I stayed in Magenta and met the Israelis, and this was filling up my whole life in the meantime.

Ezra: How did you, who did not know the meaning of *Eretz Yisrael*, regard everything the Israelis were doing? From your standpoint, was it just another job for them, or did it have special meaning for them? From your perspective at that time.

Dina: Since I had believed in human beings from an early age, people were some sort of a substitute for God. I do not need to tell you how disappointed I was in this "God" during the war. There were exceptions, a very few, but with most people that I met, I came to know all of their weaknesses and all of their lower aspects. There were those few who elevated. However, in most cases, I had a very low opinion of human beings; and so, I did not expect anything from them when I met these *Sabra* (native Israelis) who arrived there, I did not raise them too high on a pedestal. What charmed me about them, what I was not so used to meeting in people, was that they were very normal. They were so healthy from a mental standpoint, and that appealed to me very much. And the fact that people were willing to come from reasonable and healthy homes and do something for these troubled individuals who had survived the war with all of their mental baggage, with all of the most terrible things; even to listen to them, impressed me.

A person who came with Bach and Mozart records—that I considered being very normal. Because after the war was over, I prayed that I would once again feel stirred by the sight of a dead person, because I had become so used to dead people. In Warsaw there had been human skulls rolling on the streets; you could have practically kicked them. They did not bury people. And I had lain next to a dead person who made this kind of noise when the air was squeezed out of him. When you have such close encounters with death, you find yourself beyond; you are beyond fear; you are beyond excitement. So what was important for me was to have normal human feelings again; that I would be able to be amazed by music; that I could be filled with wonder about something that meets human norms.

Because what had happened to me was not normal. These young men, first of all, they had about them this peacefulness, this serenity. They were hurrying, but not in a wicked way. They also knew how to listen on their way; and they took an accordion with them to the camp and played music for us.

And they helped us regain our health with the aid of exercises. They were different. They also knew how to place themselves at a bit of distance; they did not mix so much with the immigrants. They needed the distance in order to maintain the discipline. They knew who they were dealing with, and they knew that people were stealing, and that people were prepared to con each other, Because this was how they had survived for so many years, and it was difficult to suddenly get rid of it. They needed the discipline because they had to take these people on the ships and they knew the conditions; and they had no authority—they were not policemen; they did not have sticks. It was only their words and this distance that could cause the immigrants to respect them and therefore help them. And they did it with great wisdom. So, when they kept their distance from the immigrants, it was not because of their vanity and feelings of superiority, but rather because of this basic need.

Ezra: Do you recall any incidents, meetings or occasions in which these *shlichim* used certain words that made an impression on you?

Dina: Bezalel used Yiddish in his speeches. He had not known the language when he first arrived. The Yiddish he used lacked prepositions and conjunctions. He wanted very much for people to regain their human condition as soon as possible. A young woman there did not behave herself. So he stood up in front of perhaps 500 people and gave a speech in Yiddish. And he said something like, "You are not good; you will lie by me the whole night." He meant that if she did not behave herself, he would imprison her for a whole night. The whole camp burst into laughter. This kind of laughter was as if it was the result of the devil tickling you. It was not laughter that came out of joy; it was laughter because he had made a mistake. And here you could see how much they longed for the commander to make a mistake. But he did not mind it. When thefts occurred, he stood up and said—if you will steal things; you will dig an entire hole and bury yourselves. This was the Yiddish he spoke. Later, some fellows collected all of his catchwords and gave it to him as a present. And so, together with the reproaches, there was also love; there was a wish to repair. Someone once said that they wished to bring people who would already have the feeling of Israel, because it was vital to bring people to Israel.

Through them, I began to love Israel very much, without even seeing it. I felt the smell of everything that was going on there without actually being in the place. Because do not forget that I had spent a year with them. There was someone there by the name of Avrum, who used to twirl the hair on his head. He ordered food from me and was responsible for organizing it on the ships. We used to discuss how much food would be needed for a few days, and if there were older people, that perhaps their diet should be softened; you could not cook on the ship. He was a farmer; he was like a tree that grows, and then they told this 'tree' to go and fetch immigrants. For him, this was a short break from farming. He had to come, take the immigrants and arrange food.

Ezra: And that is how you regarded them?

Dina: This is how I saw them. I want to say that Bezalel was different not only in his dealings with me. He was different from the others; he was more European. I suffered a great deal at first from the fact that he never offered me my coat and opened a door for me. He then explained to me that in Israel it would have been considered an insult to a woman if he were to hand her coat to her because this sense of equality was so developed in Israel. "In the Kibbutz, if I were to offer a coat to a girl or open a door for her, she would say, 'What? I can't do it by myself, and therefore need your help?'" These sorts of manners. With that, he was still less coarse than others, compared to someone who could, for example, bump into you and not say excuse me. Things like saying hello and goodbye did not exist for most of them. Later, when I arrived at the Kibbutz, I saw where this was coming from. I would get up in the morning, and no one would say 'good morning' to me, as if it was foul language. This is something I had difficulty getting used to. Besides, I felt like Methuselah next to them. I had gone through so much that they may have needed twenty lifetimes to go through the same experiences. On the other hand, I was a Hebrew student and a trainee in manners; they applied distance but I, on the other hand, could have been their grandmother in terms of life experience. They were so fresh.

Ezra: Did they feel that, in comparison to you and the rest of the camp, they were young? Inexperienced? Insecure?

Dina: They were scared; they did not know how to handle the whole thing. Suppose they caught someone stealing, they could not easily accuse the person, because they knew what his background was. People used to steal bread and put it under the blankets, and it would rot. This was very unpleasant. But they could not scold such a person; they did not know how to handle it. And there were all sorts of other phenomena. Look, this was a camp of different individuals who had gone through death and had no idea what to expect. Not everyone knew where they were heading and what was guiding them. A young person with no family was different to someone who already had a wife and a child. It was already 1945-1946, and children had been born in the camps. Children had also been born on ships. The war's survivors were so alone and longing for intimacy, that they connected with each other, because they had no one else. So this called for a different approach. There were times when Bezalel did not leave the camp for fear that they would steal blankets from the storage rooms. There were others who did an excellent job but wished to enjoy themselves as well. So we went to operas, we went to the theatre, but there were also those who arrived with a precise aim and did not leave the camp because they were afraid that the blankets would be stolen. And what did the thieves do with the blankets? They sold them; they turned them into coats.

Ezra: And you continued to be in charge of the camp's food storage and in charge of preparing food for the ships. The other immigrants, the newcomers, understood your status. There was no element of, "What is she doing there?"

Dina: I was jealous of them for arriving and traveling on while I remained. Our camp was about arriving, waiting and going, and I stayed on. We were a whole group there. Those who later went to Hamadia; we went there because of Avraham Zakai. He himself did not go to Hamadia, but he influenced them. I was also amongst the candidates to go to Hamadia, but I later strayed and went to Hulata. This was a group where one was in charge of the beds; another woman was in charge of sewing all sorts of things; and I was responsible for the food. There was another woman there who had trained to be a nurse on a ship because you could not travel without a nurse. So she was not a certified nurse, but she had studied with one.

The Transition Camp in Metaponto and the Immigration to Israel

Ezra: When did you begin to feel that finally, you too were starting to prepare yourself towards immigrating?

Dina: I was ready the whole time. I was not complaining or using pressure. I wanted only one thing that when Bezalel went, I would travel with him. I came to Arazi and told him that I wanted to go with Bezalel to Germany so that he could meet my parents. He said fine, we prepared ourselves, and I wrote a letter to my parents. But a week later the order arrived—you are going to Israel. In November 1946 we went to Metaponto in the south of Italy. This was a transit camp. It had several long buildings; there was a pool with water and a place to cook. We were meant to be there for just a few days. Everyone who had arrived there stayed for a few days and then boarded a ship. The ship arrived, and everything was fine, and we started to prepare ourselves. Suddenly, "the Old Man" tells Bezalel that he must board the ship, but that I have to stay behind, because there is not enough room. And he says that anyhow he did not think that it would be a good idea for the two of us to travel together. Edna Sereni was there too, and I approach her and tell her, "But we agreed that I would go with him." She then says, "Arazi has experience; you will go with the second ship. All sorts of things can happen on a ship; someone might be jealous thinking that you enjoy favouritism, why should we put that person to a test?" So Bezalel boarded the ship. This was a Swedish ship. After a while, he disembarked, because they made a calculation that they would not have enough people on the second ship.

Ezra: Were you angry with him for not disobeying?

Dina: No. It was an order. Arazi gave his orders, and no one argued with him.

Ezra: But still, sometimes there are expectations. And you were not angry?

Dina: No. Later on, there were moments during our travels when I was angry. But when he boarded the ship? No. I stood on the side and prepared hot chocolate for anyone who boarded. When he boarded, he boarded, and that was it. When he disembarked, he had with him this brown suede sweater that I had bought him as a present, and the sweater fell into the water. So Edna Sereni was very concerned about this sweater; that such a lovely sweater had been ruined. So I tell her, do not worry about the sweater, the main thing is that he is here. Then we had to wait again, because the ship that was due to arrive had broken down on the way. In the end, I spent three months in this camp instead of six days. The situation there was of absolute famine, due to the fact that not enough food had arrived, it being only a transit camp. We mainly ate goulash soup without any meat and with lots of paprika, because we had there a Hungarian cook. It was a delightful soup. I remember that during one of the meals, Bezalel added a piece of cheese to the soup and came to share it with me, and it tasted like the most delicious steak. We danced there endlessly in circles because we had to discharge our energies somehow. There was no food, so we danced; we danced the whole time. It was like a *dybbuk*,[48] this dance. It exhausted all of our energies.

Ezra: Was this a dance that came from *Eretz Yisrael*?

Dina: Yes, some of the folks organized it.

---

48 Dybbuk, in Jewish folklore, is a malevolent wandering spirit that possesses the body of a living person, until exorcized.

Ezra: They used to say that the *halutzim*[49] danced in *Emek Yisrael* (Jezreel Valley), not because of their wish to dance, but rather because of their wish to forget all of their troubles.

Dina: Precisely. They were the dance organizers and leaders. Because those 'skeletons' (survivors) did not have much strength. And if you could see how enthusiastically they all danced! It was a most unusual thing. I think, if only they had recorded it and could show now how people danced back then. I do not believe that people ever danced this way in Israel itself. And then came the moment when we boarded the ship, Shabtai Luzinski.[50] I then went into emergency mode. For eight whole days, Bezalel neither approached me nor recognized me. When I would sometimes climb up to the upper deck, he would say: go down quickly, so that no one sees you. I was furious the entire journey. I told myself that I wanted no partnership with such a person.

Ezra: Dina as one of the immigrants. I want to know what went on, from your point of view, on the Shabtai Luzinski.

Dina: We use rubber boats to get to the ship. Every boat has in it thirty people with their bags. We board the ship using a rope ladder. We had not been trained to do this. Inside, arguments had already begun about which bunk each one would get hold of. According to my experience, I knew that higher up was the best, even though the way down was long, and if you needed to reach the bathrooms, it was an agonizing hike. There were about seven stories there, and about sixty centimeters of air between the bunks; you could

---

49 Haluzim—pioneers in the act of settling Israel.

50 The Shabtai Luzinski ship had upon it 823 people, including 173 that joined during the journey. For further reading about the Shabtai Luzinski ship please see the appendix entitled, "The Immigrants' Ship Shabtai Luzinski."

hardly sit up. And that meant that you had to do almost everything lying down. I got hold of the highest spot near the deck. This whole group that was traveling with me, most of us were high up. And this was not due to favouritism; we simply thought that this was the best place. Later on, it turned out that this was not necessarily the case, because the hot air rose up in that direction. Downstairs was a total mess. Because until you sat everyone down… people are human beings after all. And we had already set sail, and outside there was a terrible storm. And I knew that, in fact, there was no one on this ship that I could really count on. I knew that if there had been an Italian captain there, we might be able to arrive in one piece. Because after all, the fellows from Israel had never actually navigated a full-size ship. But I was not scared. People had no idea that the young people leading us did not have even an ounce of experience. We reach the middle of the sea, and on top of how crowded we already are, another small ship arrives, transfers more immigrants to us, and sails back. This was the situation. Those people had no room at all. They were all on the deck, and I feared that the food would not suffice, since we had prepared food for a certain number of people. There was fear that we would not have enough water and there was a longer queue to the bathrooms and to everything else. This increased the tension and people started quarreling amongst themselves. In the meantime, someone went into labor. The doctor was extremely weak and vomited the whole time; they had to carry him on their hands and bring him to the woman who was giving birth, and he gave orders what to do. Everyone was vomiting, and the ship was swaying from side to side. You offered food, and half of it was spilled out. This ship was very much like a nutshell; so much courage was needed to take us on board something like this.

Ezra: Were there incidents, on the ship, of people being in a bad state and lashing out?

Dina: As far as I know, there were none on our ship. As I've told you, I was practically in prison and was not allowed to go up. Later on, I asked myself, what wrong had I done? What crime had I committed? By the end, no one cared if I was his girlfriend or not. People started laughing at the whole thing because they knew that we were in a relationship. So they said that he probably found some prettier girl on deck.

I decided that probably the mentality of Israelis was different from ours, and that this was not going to work. This is what I decided during the journey. I did not eat for seven or eight days; I did not sleep the entire time, and that person did not come to ask if I were alive or dead. Someone must have informed him that I was alive. However, to share the rest of my life with such a person? No way.

Ezra: Were there other sailors on this ship?

Dina: There was Ossi Ravid and another one, a redhead from Kibbutz Ayelet Hashahar. I think there were three or four of them and that's it. There was also David Ben-Nun. There were not many. Yudaleh led the second ship and traveled back to the shores of Italy. There was some kind of a system; they did not tell us about it in advance. We did not know.

Ezra: Did those who were already on board ask why they were bringing more?

Dina: They did not take it well, because there was no room and we still had to share somehow with the newcomers. And they too were not prepared for this. I was not on deck; most of the time I was lying down, half conscious, in my bunk. I would only get up to see if the food was well organized, because I had written on the boxes their order according to the days. I wanted to see how that went. When the fellows returned from a trip such as this one, I placed a box, just for them, filled with goodies. I never wrote what was inside the box so that when they opened it they would be surprised. They always thanked me for the surprises I left for them inside. There was sweetened condensed milk; there was chocolate; there were all sorts of things. I used to always ask them how the food was, and they always replied that it sufficed and that there were no blunders. And now, suddenly, we had to reduce the food and water rations because of all the additional people. And our trip was much longer as well, in order to mislead the British. We pretended to sail in the direction of Egypt and later sailed towards Nitzanim.[51]

Ezra: When do you begin to see the shores of Israel? Do you speak about the British pursuit? Do you hate the British? The same British soldiers who in fact had liberated Jews? Does the strangeness of this fact influence the immigrants? Do they give it expression?

Dina: I think that, from this perspective, I had the most difficulty because I had worked with the British soldiers and loved them very much. Very, very much. I had also been lucky and worked with very nice people. They were so generous and so kind and so liberating and now, all of a sudden, I saw that we feared them very much. There was already fear of them finding out in Italy. And there on the ship, when we heard a noise from above, it caused fear. When we saw an

---

51 Kibbutz Nitzanim is located in southern Israel, between the cities of Ashkelon and Ashdod, on the Nitzanim dunes.

airplane, we had to hide. All the people who were on deck had no physical place to go to, but they all went below and huddled together, a fact that brought about tension, but this was already towards the end. We arrived at Nizanim Beach at three in the morning. We did not see the shores of Israel, as it was dark and so stormy we could not see a thing.

We nearly reach the beach. The silence is complete, and you do not see a thing. The ship can't reach the beach; we are about two hundred meters away from it, and the waves are crashing all the way up, and the order is to jump into the water. Who's going to jump into the water? Are they crazy? To jump into the water in February, into the freezing and the frightening waves? The fellows say that there is no choice; and that we have to jump. In the meantime, a group of *palmachniks*,[52] who had gathered together in Nizanim, in order to welcome us, tie a cable all the way to the ship so that if anyone falls, they'll have something to hold onto. There was a seven-year-old boy there who jumped first, and everyone followed him.

This boy was Ossi Ravid's brother. Ossi was not a *palmachnik*; he served in the brigade. Knowing that his younger brother had survived, he had searched for the boy until he found him. This boy used to play chess in a most phenomenal way.

---

52 Palmachnik—a member of the *Palmach* (acronym for Plugot Mahatz; lit. "strike forces"), the elite fighting force of the Haganah, the underground army of the Jewish people in Israel during the period of the British Mandate for Palestine. The Palmach was the spearhead of the fighting units of the forming State of Israel during the war of independence and played a major role in defending the Jewish community. The "spirit of the Palmach" was that of friendship, allegiance to the mission and keeping the purity of Arms. Palmach fighters, both men and women, were known to be unconventional and creative in their ways. At most it had some 6,000 troops, 20% of whom were killed in action. The Palmach was founded in 1941 and merged into the IDF in 1948, during this time it carried out most of the important missions of the young arm forces of the arising State of Israel.

He was probably a very brave boy and more mature than others his age, and he jumped first into the water. After he had jumped, the adults were not comfortable seeing that a boy had jumped, while they had not.

I did not know how to swim; I was scared to death of the water. Bezalel knew it. I had a small nylon bag that I had taken with me on the journey, so that if I would not be able to take my things, I would at least have a change of underwear or something. This bag was tied to my hand. Those who came from the beach climbed up on the ship, as well, in order to help. Israel Wein from Ra'anana was there, and Bezalel told him: "You see this young woman? Give her a small push into the water. She will not go on her own; she is my girlfriend."

Israel pushed, and I flew overboard and found myself head down in the water. All he could see was my bag, which saved me because, had it not been for this nylon bag, he might not have found me. He took my hand and led me through the water in that horrible storm. I swallowed a lot of water and, by the time I reached the beach, it was the peak of everything; I was unable to handle any more of it. I lay down on the sand, and he said to me, my friend, you cannot faint now, only later, there is no time. And you will be surprised at what such words can do. He told me that I could not faint then because we had to reach the Kibbutz, but that I would be able to faint there. These words encouraged me, and I remained conscious. He brought me to the Kibbutz, placed me in a room; and someone brought me dry clothes.

My parcel was wet; it had no value. I came out in different clothes. They collected us in order to take us out of the Kibbutz as soon as possible. Some of the people had already left; they'd been taken to Beer Tuvia. However, they did not succeed in removing us because the British had detected the movement in the meantime and arrived with airplanes and boats. The storm was so strong that one of their boats turned over and three British soldiers drowned. No one from our ship drowned; they all left by jumping. Bezalel was the funniest, because he could not walk on the sand without shoes and therefore jumped with a swimsuit and shoes. They were given clothes later.

And you ask yourself, where did these people who greeted us find their ideas? When the British soldiers started to circle us, those who came to pick us up built a fire and started throwing their identity certificates into it and, when asked, everyone said they were Jews from *Eretz Yisrael*. The British soldiers took us to their trucks; 250 managed to escape. We, Bezalel and I, together with those who came to fetch us, did not manage to escape.

The Deportation to the Internment Camp in Cyprus

Dina: The British soldiers took us in automobiles. They had to force us because we refused to climb in. They struggled in order to get us into the trucks. The road was long and cold. We traveled the whole night from Nizanim to Haifa. We arrived in the morning completely frozen. We did not speak, but cuddled close together in order to fight the cold. I had a windbreaker and wrapped myself inside it. We were hungry and thirsty. When we arrived, we received a severe beating from the British soldiers because we refused to come out.

We were forced onto a deportation ship while hungry, tired and angry. And I saw Haifa for the first time from a distance, from a deportation ship. I was already so close and once again traveling back; so I began to cry. How could I be so close and so far away? I had no idea for how long I am going to Cyprus.[53] We had already succeeded to arrive on the shores of Israel, and I had already spoken to someone in Hebrew at the Kibbutz, and I had already smelled something, and yet they were taking us away.

We were on the deportation ship; I made friends with a girl who is still my friend to this very day, Batia Lerman. There were lots of Israelis there. If you looked well, you could detect them. There were even those who received an order to travel together with us because they had to stay in Cyprus for the purpose of teaching and training us, and that was a good way to get there. We were on our journey, and we started throwing things at the British soldiers, cursing them, speaking to them not nicely; it was a small revenge.

Ezra: Did some kind of hate develop towards those British soldiers or towards the British Empire?

Dina: I do not know if the Israelis hated the British soldiers. They treated them as those who were carrying out orders. When we were on the ship, we threw a shoe at a British soldier, and he brought it back and said you will need this for walking. And I said to him, thank you very much; you are very kind, but look at what you are doing to us. And he said, do you

---

53 The internment camps in Cyprus were built by the British government between August 1946 and November 1949, in order to detain Jewish immigrants arriving to Israel, as a means of discouraging the Jewish community from continuing to operate the illegal immigration. By the middle of 1947, there were already around 15,000 immigrants in the camps in Cyprus. The status of those detained was one of prisoners of war.

think that I enjoy it? This is the last thing I want to do; I would rather be in London now. Do you think that this is my job? That this is what I want to do with my life? He never left my side and wanted to justify himself the whole time. I told him, you know, I came from Germany with so much love for the British soldiers; they liberated me; look what you are doing to me; you are killing the image I hold of you. This big and beautiful nation—how can you be so beautiful over there and so ugly here. And he explained to me what was going on—I am the same person, and I could have been in Germany now, liberating Jews and offering food to the refugees, and now I shall have to beat you up for remaining alive and coming to Israel.

We were on our way to Cyprus, and soon we already needed to disembark. We clung to one another and said that we were not coming down. They had a method—they closed the deck with canvas and started throwing bombs filled with tear gas at us. We had amongst us pregnant women and small children, and so we let them leave first; but how long can you hold on? We were choking. We started to come out, and the soldiers stood in two rows, and we spat at them and pushed them while walking between those rows. They were so disciplined and did not respond. After we left, they aired the place and led us back to the same location since there was no other place for us. They said that the commander of the action wanted to speak to us. He came down and opened by saying, "I am sorry I have to do this." How can you relate to such contradictions? You cannot hate him. He looked so elegant and so nice and at the same time he had given the order to throw tear gas at us.

Ezra: Did it look like a lie?

Dina: It did not look false. He seemed genuinely sorry for having to do this. Later, I went over to him and said, "You know you made a farce out of yourself? How dare you speak like this to people? Do you know who they are? Do you know what they went through? And you say that you are sorry for giving the order to throw tear gas at them? To them, these gases are associated with other gases." So he said, "I received an order." I told him, "You can always refuse an order." So he said, "If I refuse an order, there will be someone else here who'll be worse." Anyway, till the end, I did not feel hatred towards them, in spite of all the beatings I received, and I received beatings by clubs. I also saw how they pulled Bezalel and beat him up. This was a very unpleasant sight, to see how my 'God' was being humiliated.

Ezra: If there was no hatred, then what?

Dina: First of all, understanding the situation. I understood the situation. They were caught in a trap. I understood that they could not give the Jews freedom to enter because they feared the Arabs. They did not want to anger the Arab world.

Ezra: What did you know about Arabs and Jews?

Dina: I knew a great deal, because I had worked with British soldiers, and this issue had erupted before I came to Israel. I had asked questions before arriving in Israel. I was always familiar with international politics because the territory always interested me, and I wanted to know where I stood. I did not hate the British soldier; I felt sorry for him. I know that he did not do it with joy.

We arrived in Cyprus. They placed the Israelis who came in a separate tent, not together with everyone else. And they created for me, in the tent, a partition made of two blankets and that is where I slept. I had many moral guards over there. And the fellows, those who were meant to act, they immediately divided them. There was order in Cyprus. There were schools; there was gymnastics, and there were a military organization and movements that operated and acted inside the camps.

In the meantime, a big drama was taking place in Cyprus, because Yossale Dror had received an order to blow up one of these deportation ships. There were three deportation ships, and the whole time they (the Palyam unit) strove to destroy these ships, so that they would not have the ability to deport. Perhaps there would be other ships but, until they arrived, the ones that were there needed to be put out of action. They tried several times but were not too successful.

Yossale had to reach a ship that was anchored at a certain distance from the beach. The British soldiers knew about these intentions and, therefore, distanced the ships from the shore. This ship was pretty far away, and he had to swim to it, attach explosives and return to the camp. When he was already close to the ship and had almost attached the explosives, one of the soldiers, who was looking for a bag, bent down on the deck and detected him. They chased and caught him. The ship was not harmed, and Yossale was placed in prison. Later, a girl named Raissa, who was a nurse there, entered, in order to visit him, and succeeded to release him. To conduct the same act of blowing up a deportation ship, Ori Yoffe, who was Bezalel's direct commander, appointed Bezalel.

The Return to Israel and the Blowing Up of the Empire Rival Deportation Ship

Dina: We were sent back to Israel as part of the quota, three weeks after our arrival. We returned with explosives that I carried on my body. Suddenly, I was a pregnant woman.

Ezra: Did you ask about the belt of explosives you were wearing?

Dina: I do not recall asking questions. They told me to wear it, and that was it—I wore it. I was glad to be going to Israel. I already felt like someone who had come from Israel to help the immigrants, because I dealt with issues that were typically handled by the Israelis. I took the explosives because we thought that I would seem less suspicious, masquerading as a pregnant woman. So they dressed me up as a pregnant woman. What was rather dangerous, and I only found out about it later, was that earlier, on the ship, we had thrown shoes at the soldiers, and I had personally spoken with them. Then, we returned on the same ship, without giving this any thought. And I left with an amusing certificate—I was Avraham Razal, who was forty. So I was a man, nearly twice my age, and carrying explosives as a pregnant woman. All of this together.

I board the ship, and a soldier is wandering around there, and I see that he recognizes me. He approaches me and says, you have grown fat so quickly. He does not understand how I could have become so big. I pretend not to understand and make myself scarce as soon as possible, so that he won't see me again. On a ship that big, it was possible to vanish amongst the immigrants. They removed my 'pregnancy' and quickly went off with the explosives. There were fellows there who carried nets. The camp in Cyprus had ropes tied between the tents. The guys made everything out of these ropes—furniture, clothes, blankets, nets for games.

However, we needed these nets for a different purpose. They brought along the nets but did not know about their intended use. They were told that the nets were required for a game of handball. When we got to the ship, Bezalel saw there a group of quality fellows from HaShomer HaTzair.[54] Young men, each better than the other. He started arranging for them to sit next to him. He told them that he had been given a mission to go down into the belly of the ship to see what was happening there so that they would later be able to blow it up. He did not tell them the whole truth. He only told them that his mission was to check the insides of the ship in order to find out if it can be blown up.

He was afraid that they would not help him, because who would want to blow up a ship, together with its passengers. It was only a two-day trip from Cyprus to Israel. The British feared an attempt to penetrate the lower parts of the ship, so they placed a net over the deck, and the British soldiers patrolled there and watched what was happening with us, and the deck was fortified with iron poles. How would it be possible to remove the poles without the soldiers noticing? They began organizing dances and public singing, and these muffled the noise of the banging.

I chatted with the soldiers to prevent them from noticing what we were doing. And people began looking at me skeptically; how come a young woman is socializing with soldiers and talking with them? One of the officers asked me, why are they dancing like this? I told him that this was a religious ceremony; that this is how they give expression to their spiritual energy, and this takes a while and must not be stopped in the middle. The sorts of ideas that enter people's minds at

---

54 HaShomer HaTzair (translating as The Young Guard) is a Socialist-Zionist, secular Jewish youth movement founded in 1913 in Galicia, Austria-Hungary, and was also the name of the group's political party in the pre-1948 British Mandate of Palestine.

a time of need are quite something… some kind of correct intuition, and this also helped us a great deal later on. Bezalel succeeded to raise the iron net and enter inside. He rolled down the net of ropes and with its help managed to climb down. Two fellows held the net from above as if it were a rope ladder. He went down and checked and saw that he could not place the explosives then; he would have to do it later, when we were closer to the harbor. Because he remembered Patria.[55] He did not trust the explosives and preferred to plant them at the last moment. We were approaching the port, and he needed to climb down and place them at the last minute, so that there would be only the smallest chance of blowing it up together with the people.

People started to disembark, and he was still downstairs. We had agreed that as soon as he heard a specific song he would place the explosives and climb out. Half of the people had already left, and he was still downstairs, and we started singing that song and the British started saying "come along," and I tell them, "But I told you that the dance must be completed," but that did not help, and they began beating us up. And the British were shouting that we must finish. At the last moment, Bezalel came out, and he had to reinforce that iron net so that no one would notice. He took with him the safety catch of the bomb. I had already descended before that, and Orri Yoffe was there, and I gave him a particular

---

55 Patria was a British deportation ship that carried immigrants from three ships that had been captured in November 1940. The ship was carrying the illegal immigrants to Mauritius. Wishing to delay the deportation, the Haganah planted a bomb on the ship while it was anchored at Haifa harbor. Their intention was to cause slight damage, but the explosion was quite large; the ship sank on November 25, 1940 and took with it more than two hundred immigrants and fifty British soldiers.

sign. Later, Bezalel gave him the safety catch as proof that he had pulled it out from the explosives.[56]

Avoiding the Detention Camp in Atlit

Dina: When we come out of the ship, Bezalel tells me, "I will hide somehow; I am not going to Atlit.[57] I don't know what you'll do; just don't get to Atlit. You don't have a certificate, and that will immediately lead them to the explosion." Indeed, I could hardly enter with the certificate I had, made out in the name of Avraham Razal, a forty-year-old man.

And Bezalel did disappear immediately. They had arranged for him a porter's costume and given him a sack to carry. They were unable to remove me like that. I entered the bus to Atlit. I thought to myself, what do I do? How do I get away from here? On both sides of the bus, there is a close escort of British motorcycles. I must go over to the driver and have a chat with him; my Hebrew is not that good, but I do speak it.

At a certain point, Bezalel had gotten tired of speaking English with me, and said he would only talk to me in Hebrew: "Whatever you will understand, you will understand." In the beginning, it had been a monologue; later I had started answering him. And how did he propose to

---

56 On April 3, 1947, the Empire Rival, a ship used by the British to deport immigrants to Cyprus, exploded far out in the sea. The Palmach soldier, Bezalel Drori, had planted explosives inside the ship. This happened a day after the immigrants were taken off the ship and while it was on route to Alexandria. The charge exploded and caused heavy damage to the ship.

57 The Atlit detention camp was established by the British Mandate for Palestine authorities at the end of the 1930s. It served to detain over 40,000 Jewish refugees, preventing them from entering Palestine. The camp was active until the establishment of the State of Israel in 1947.

me? I did not know that his name was Bezalel. They called him Yashka; he gave himself his uncle's name, so that if anyone would inquire about the family, they would discover a relative of his. And true enough, someone did hear the name and found a relative with the help of this name. I did not know his name—he had not told me yet. Once, when we were still in Italy, we sat on the beach, and he drew the letters D.D. on the sand and asked me whether I liked the combination of D.D. I told him that any monogram with double letters is pretty. And he said, "Your name one day will be D.D.," and this was the first clue.[58]

I did not speak Hebrew well. My Hebrew was rather basic. So I go over to the driver and tell him, "I not Atlit." And he replies, "Of course you are not Atlit." So I tell him, "I not want Atlit." That is how we carry on the conversation. He understands what I want, but tells me that he cannot help since the police escort is surrounding us. He says, "The police are on both sides, but I will not 'notice' anything you do." We arrive at Atlit; people start leaving the bus, and I start walking towards the back of the bus. I reach the last bench and think to myself, what will happen if I hide under the last bench? I push myself under that last bench. I find a sack there; I was wearing a white sweater and covered myself with the sack, thinking that perhaps they will not notice me. The whole bus empties out; in comes a Brit holding a lantern; it's already evening; he looks under all the benches and does not notice me; he takes a seat and rides with the bus, and he keeps talking the whole time. I think to myself, what will happen if, God forbid, I need to sneeze? But he leaves the bus, and I continue to lie hidden. When the bus stops, I come out from my hiding place, fearing that the driver will leave and

---

58 D.D. stands for Dina Drori. Drori was the name Bezalel's family adopted after immigrating to Israel; the Hebrew version of the original family name, Freiman.

lock me on the bus if he does not know that I am there. And he starts laughing—such a liberating laughter. He is so glad that he has managed to trick the British soldiers, and that one woman has not entered the Atlit camp. It's the day before Passover eve; he stops at the station, and all of the drivers come out, and I am so dirty and with this sack; and they start to hug me and kiss me and say, "How wonderful that this girl managed to trick the British."

And the driver? They made him a national hero. His name was Katz, and he lived on 15 Ruth Street in Haifa. He had a baby who had been born one week earlier. I did not have a certificate. He decided to take me home, but before he entered the house, he asked me to wait so that he could prepare his wife. He went into the house and prepared her, and she came out. They bathed me and dressed me in a clean gown and gave me food. I went to sleep; the baby cried the whole night, and it did not bother me. The following morning, I ate a grapefruit for the first time in my life. It had such a unique taste that until this day, whenever I eat a grapefruit, I always remember the taste of that first one.

I stayed with them for the duration of the Passover holiday. I could not obtain a certificate, because the offices were closed. There was no telephone; I had no one I could notify. They hosted me warmly for four days. Later, Katz arranged a forged certificate for me, in which I was called Dina Minzberg. This was my real name, but the certificate was not official. And this is how I received a forged certificate with my real name. In the meantime, they took Bezalel to a hotel in Haifa, and nothing was announced yet about the ship. Only the following morning, messages went out saying that the ship sailed, and that there was an explosion when it was mid-way.

During the time of immigration

Bezalel during the time
of immigration

In the Magenta transit camp, creating
a relief of the map of Israel

The food storage in the
Magenta transit camp**

Preparing hammocks in the Magenta transit camp**

The immigrants' ship Shabtai Luzinski**

One of the boats used to bring the immigrants'
belongings from the Shabtai Luzinski ship to shore**

Immigrants from the Shabtai Luzinski ship reach the shore**

The immigration ship, Shabtai Luzinski**

The detention camp in Cyprus, 1947**

The deportation ship, Empire Rival**

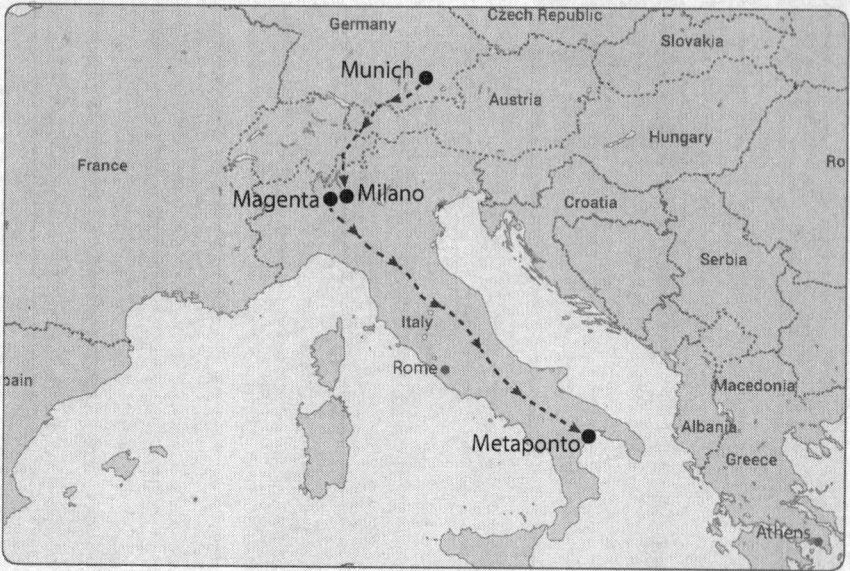

The journey from Munich to Italy

The course of the Shabtai Luzinski immigration ship **- -**
and the deportation ship, Empire Rival **- -**

Chapter Four
The Family

The Wedding

Dina: In the meantime, Bezalel had arrived in Ra'anana and did not know where I was. He called various sources to see whether I had reached Atlit, but no one knew. And his parents, Shoshana and Abraham Freiman, as well as his friends, started to say—what kind of a groom are you? You brought a bride and lost her on the way...

Ezra: The parents knew that he had a girlfriend?

Dina: Of course. We wrote from Italy and sent photographs. It had already been decided. We did not get married there because we wanted them to participate in the celebration. So, once Passover ended, Katz and his wife gave me money and put me on a bus to Ra'anana. While travelling, I saw the sprinklers revolving. It was spring. The day was a bit hot. I saw the orchards on the way and fell in love—in a way that only a person who has waited for that moment for two thousand years could—with the trees, with the land. And it was the kind of feeling that makes you want to never stop singing. To this day, I have this feeling of loving everything that grows here and lives here. I have never seen before such water sprinklers. In Italy, they had taught us the song, "Mayim, Mayim, Mayim, Mayim, Ho Mayim Bessasson" (water, water, water,

water, hey water with joy). And I could hear the song in my head, and I suddenly realized where the words were coming from. I wanted the journey to continue for a long time, but time passed quickly and I was suddenly in Ra'anana.

I know that something unknown awaits me. I am on my way to meet people whom I do not know; I don't know how they will welcome me. Before I departed, Bezalel had told me that his mother asked him to do whatever is needed for this country, but not to bring home a new immigrant. Perhaps if they had not told him this, it would have never occurred to him. I arrive in Ra'anana. I have the address. I already know his name. Before leaving the ship, he had told me his exact name and where he lived, so I would know where to go.

I arrived at 18 Maccabi Street and knocked on the door and a young man, who looked a bit like Bezlalel, came out; it was Bezalel's eighteen-year-old brother, Aharoni. There was also a relative, who always used to come over for Passover; she looked at me and asked me where my luggage was. I arrived by ship, I came to Israel, where was my luggage? I do not recall if I even had a bag. Katz' wife had given me one of her dresses and some underwear. I arrived with, perhaps, one small bag. So I told her that the luggage was still on the ship and was due to arrive. Aharoni knew that I arrived by ship and he assumed that I was probably tired and cold; he suggested I go have a rest and covered me with a duvet. There was a heat wave. I thought this was how one was supposed to behave and was embarrassed to remove it.

Bezalel's father was in the shop; his mother had gone out, as well, and Bezalel was out again looking for me; travelling to all sorts of places. In the evening, Bezalel's father and mother returned and welcomed me in a very nice way in comparison to what I was expecting, as a new immigrant; his father began inquiring about my place of origin, wanted to know my name, and my parents' occupation; this was what interested him. And suddenly, Bezalel arrived. They put me in a cupboard, in order to play with him a bit. He enters, and they ask, so what? Where is she? And they start laughing at him, for being the sort of man who does not search enough for me. After a while, I came out of the closet, and there was great rejoicing.

I still have not come to a final conclusion about what to do with myself. After that trip on the ship, I had thought it would be good to get to know one another against the background of Israel. That we would go together to a Kibbutz. That I would go to Messilot or to Yakum, where I had two cousins. My cousin from Yakum had already come to visit me. I talked to Bezalel about it and told him that perhaps it would be nice if I could get to know him a bit against the background of Israel; that we should not rush into the marriage. But his mother said that if we are to go to Hulata, it would be better if we were married. She put us in a situation we didn't know how to handle.

His mother then went to Tel Aviv and bought fabrics; she hired a woman to cook for the wedding; they set a date; they did everything without consulting with us. Not that I was upset by this; I am only saying that I had had this thought of getting to know Bezalel a bit more in Israel, because there, in Europe, he could have been from a different planet; whereas here we were more equal. Because I was already an Israeli. Do not forget that I was a little different from other refugees. I had not been in a concentration camp; I had experienced all sorts of things, and I believed in my own strengths. During the war, I struggled; I did not drift.

It matures you. I wanted, when it was possible, to consider things, not to fall under them. because up until then, I had been pushed the whole time; I mean, destiny pushed me.

We set the wedding date for May 29. It coincided with the eve of the Shavuot holiday (Pentecost). We prepared the yard by ourselves, because it was like a jungle. We worked full days to prepare the wedding. They invited 500 people. Almost all of the residents of Ra'anana were there. On the groom's side, everyone wanted to figure me out and to see what Bezalel had brought home with him; and they said that he had brought with him a *shiksseh* (a non-Jewish maid in Yiddish); they comforted his mother by saying that although I was a *goya*, I was nice all the same. This happened because they knew that I had Arian documents. I was deeply insulted. Years later, when my father arrived in Ra'anana in 1963, they understood that I was not a goya (after all, he was a rabbi).

Ezra: You arrived during the most difficult and greatest time the country had gone through, and there was a war here.

Dina: No, it was still in 1947. The anxiety of the *yishuv*[59] did not interest me at all. I was here now. I wanted to push it away from me. I came home and I wanted my home. I wanted to avoid it and to not feel it too deeply. I was very insulted when they thought I was a *goya*; you want to keep your identity. Because what is your identity? It is you. And suddenly they take it away from you. You simply cannot argue with the whole of Ra'anana. Bezalel's father wrote to Munich, because he wanted to know. Bezalel responded to this with understanding; a new immigrant arrives, and she

---

59 Jewish population of Israel prior to the establishment of the State.

has no proof with her; so, of course, the father would want to know who she is. Besides, I had so much family pride inside me that I knew that if he wrote there, nothing bad would come out of it, only good. This, as well, is something that strengthens you in all sorts of situations—the family pride. It gives you an incredible strength.

Ezra: You corresponded by letters with your family.

Dina: Yes, of course. I immediately wrote to them that we were sorry but would not hold off the wedding for their arrival, because we did not know when that would be. The wedding was a very confusing event, because Bezalel's parents invited 500 people from Ra'anana but, from my side, there were only my cousin from Yakum, Itzhak Preiss, his wife, Beatrice. Ori Yoffe, who was an envoy of the Palmach and the Palyam and sort of represented those fellows; and there was also Henia, who had arrived together with me on the ship. These were all of my guests. This was the wedding. I recall telling my sister once, that it is imperative to feel, when under the *chuppah* (the Jewish wedding canopy), that you are doing the right thing. Regarding the future, you are not responsible for all that will happen afterwards. However, at that moment, when I stood under the canopy, I consciously knew that I was doing the right thing. I told my Hana once that people cannot guarantee life for themselves, but they must feel in that moment, that this is it; that they are doing the right thing; that their choice, at that moment, is the right choice. It accompanied me through all sorts of situations that were not easy. Coming to a new land, getting married, moving on to a whole new way of life.

We did not stay long in Ra'anana after the wedding. That period of time was enchanting; the smell of the orchards intoxicated me. It caused a sensation of developing new senses. When I think about my arrival to Israel, the thoughts are always accompanied by the picture of the water sprinklers, the smell of the orchards and the bright days. It is a clarity that does not exist elsewhere. You wake up in the morning with this fierce sun. You have all these feelings moving inside you that you never had before.

In Kibbutz Hulata

Dina: We went to the Kibbutz, accompanied by the mental preparation that Bezalel had given me—that only difficulties awaited me there. Nothing good awaited me at the Kibbutz. He told me that, perhaps, he would have to leave or that he might be assigned to a task that would keep him away from home and that I needed to prepare myself to be alone amongst strangers. He prepared me for a life of daily difficulties; that I would live in difficult conditions; that we would hardly have a home; that we might need to live in a tent. They gave us a room that was not too big. The fellows who had been with Bezalel in the refugee camps arranged the room nicely, including flowers. There was a bed and a table, but the table belonged to the "community hall" and had to be returned later on. They placed it there only to prevent the new immigrant from collapsing at the sight of the room.

We had two orange crates, and they had to serve as a cupboard. I took everything for granted. Two days after we arrived, I began to work in the laundry room. A girl who had emigrated from Syria initiated me into the work but did not know how to train me. It was the first time that I had seen such a laundry room. We had to hang the laundry half wet; there was no cart, so we had to carry the laundry on our shoulders.

•

At the same time, while I was working in the laundry room, I was also accepted to work in the nursery. When I arrived there, I noticed that the caregivers collected the nappies and boiled them together with their smelly content. This caused me to approach the Kibbutz management and complain to them about the inability to create the truly clean environment needed for taking care of the babies. When I approached the lady in charge, she said to me: "Babies' poo smells; it does not stink…," and I felt as though someone had slapped me in the face. The caregivers would put the dirty nappies with all their content into a barrel and, after the laundry, the nappies came out looking rather ugly and gray. Regretfully, and with no other choice, I had to accept that lady's response.

•

My Hebrew was rather bad. I did learn some Hebrew from Bezalel, but he was not a great talker, and I did not reply. Whatever I understood was the result of wishing to understand what he was saying to me.

At the Kibbutz, there was a friend, Yedidiah, who thought I needed Hebrew lessons. But they said no, she does not deserve Hebrew lessons for no reason. So he volunteered to teach me after I finished my work. But they did not allow me to leave work an hour early. The work in the laundry room drained all of my strength. We were far from the fellows themselves, because they lived higher up the hill and we still lived below. To walk up the hill in the evening was a story in itself. Bezalel started working with the fodder, together with Shimon Nissanov, who was one of the stronger guys in Hulata, and who challenged Bezalel to match him. They would rip the grass with a scythe; Shimon would do it elegantly, as though he was dancing ballet; Bezalel would come home and fall into bed; there was no one to talk to— he did not even have enough energy to wash himself.

The water for the shower came from the Hula Lake. Since the water was not filtered, it would block the shower head. So, we used to take off the head and shower just like that— in a stream of cold water, which was a horrible experience. You would open the tap and receive a shock from the cold…These were my early experiences in the Kibbutz: The laundry room, Bezalel's and my hard work, the little learning I received from Yedidiah about the history of the land and some Hebrew. I felt thirsty to read, but the library had no books in English and, of course, none in Polish. Bezalel decided that I had probably never read in my life, because he never saw me reading a book or a newspaper. I could not read a newspaper as it was too difficult for me and I did not have books in my language. I had no book of my own, because I had only brought with me, to *Eretz Yisrael*, the dress I wore. Anyhow, this was the situation—the thirst to read, the inability to study due to the fatigue, and the disorganized process of absorption into the Kibbutz due to the fact that I arrived with Bezalel and they trusted him to do the job. But Bezalel fell off his feet each evening, because of his work and not being able to match Shimon Nissanov's ruthless pace.

These were the first months of a misguided process of absorption. Since he had already done the intake by himself abroad, there was no absorption in Israel. The landscape of the Galilee was breathtaking, but I had no time to look at it; I had no possibility; everything was so intensive. I arrived at the beginning of June 1947; I hardly had time to breathe the air before I was being given all that hard work. They let us live inside a concrete block that squeezed everything out of us, because it was so hot inside during the day and emitted even more heat during the night. Bezalel started working in fishing and I hardly ever saw him. He worked at night and slept during the day. When I returned from work, I would fall on the bed. It was like a "hot bunking."[60] They gave us a bed for two with a single mattress, because I was the only one entitled to a mattress from the Jewish Agency, so that is what they gave us. The concern for the general life of the organization was so great that, somewhere along the line, they lost the concern for the individual human being. Since Bezalel was taken for granted, they did not have to absorb him. They assumed that, since he was a member, he was naturally acquainted with all the difficulties. And I had to understand that this was how one lived on a Kibbutz.

---

60 Common military practice in which more than one person is assigned to a single bed or bunk, to reduce space.

•

After some time, I asked to be transferred, and began working in the vegetable garden of the Kibbutz. At the same time, Bezalel was working in fishing in the Hula Lake, and his and his friends' catches were excellent. Unlike me, Bezalel was happy in his work, since this was his profession and since the men used to compete to see who would fish a larger amount each time.

Another distress surfaced in the vegetable garden. My back was very sensitive, dating back to my work in the factory during the war. The work in the garden demanded lots of bending and lifting of heavy weights. I asked to be transferred to work with the young children in the kindergarten, and I became a kindergarten teacher, in charge of a group of children.

This job was to my liking, and the Kibbutz doctor shared my ideas on how to raise the children. I remember those ideas very well. For example, that there was no need to raise children with toys, because playing with them does not allow the child to connect with nature and with the sun. We used to take the children out on sunny days, and they played with the natural materials of the environment, such as soil, mud, sand, stones, leaves, and pine cones...

I was also in favour of more natural food, and translated this into offering more vegetables than meat, while the other caregivers thought that meat was the healthiest diet for a young child. Each educational idea that I wanted to implement and suggested to them, they chose to discard or to fight me on. I spent nearly two years as a caregiver with the same group of children, and became very attached to them. When our children were born, I tried to apply these educational ideas with them as well.

•

Ezra: You came from over there. And here, in Israel, it took a long time until they comprehended what had happened. Was there any girlfriend or anyone else in Hulata who listened to you? Did you tell your story? Did you want to tell it?

Dina: They did not want to know, and I was not too inclined to tell. I will tell you my deepest reason. Bezalel had been so immersed in all the stories the immigrants told him, that he mentally rejected all of this disgrace that befell the Jews. He felt personally insulted by it all. He carried some sort of feeling of collective insult for the humiliation that was done to the Jews. The humiliation hurt him most of all. I saw that this caused a physical pain in him. So, if you speak to someone who does not want to listen, when he does open up, you become closed yourself. The Israelis who lived here had so many problems of their own that they did not really want to open themselves to the problems that the new immigrants had faced overseas. Perhaps there was a feeling of guilt for not having done enough or a wish to escape these horrible things. So it was like saying: "If I do not know, then I do not have to feel."

Ezra: So you closed up because Bezalel could not take anymore?

Dina: Yes, this closedness caused a feeling of loneliness in me. On the one hand, it was the right thing to do, since upon my arrival in Israel I had built a new identity. So, perhaps, I closed the subject on purpose, without telling myself that this is what I was doing. It could have been the right kind of protection in support of the possibility of growing a new identity. If I had continued to tell and live the old identity, I would never have been able to attain what I wanted. I wanted the identity of a free person, a person who could handle the things I was facing there and then.

Ezra: Did you also want to be like other people? You saw the youth in Ra'anana, Bezalel's friends.

Dina: I did not want to be like them, but what bothered me was the lack of a shared past. I wanted to have a shared past with a particular person, so that I could say that I went to school with him, that we shared a mutual experience. Instead, I would sit there, and they would tell stories about HaMahanot HaOlim[61] and from Bezalel's classroom, and I always felt like I was an outsider. And truly, I was not a part of it. I was a foreign element. They shared experiences, even the songs they sang. I did not fully understand the words. A song is something that accompanies you, which is born out of a national or social experience. When you sing the song without being connected to its core, the words do not radiate at the same strength. I am sorry that my brother, living in Canada, will never go through this experience of becoming acquainted with the songs that were written here over the course of time. The songs we sang back then, strange as they may have sounded coming out of my mouth, and without knowing what caused their appearance, were songs of the path.

Ezra: Bezalel's friends from the Palyam used to meet? Did you have any contact with those who had been together with you in the camp?

Dina: Hardly. Some of them continued on to the Navy. He had a friend in Kibbutz Yagur, whom we visited, and he had another friend in Kibbutz Alonim.

Ezra: He took you by the hand, and showed you the country?

---

61 HaMahanot HaOlim was a Zionistic and socialistic pioneering youth movement that was founded in Tel Aviv in 1926; it later founded 40 kibbutzim around Israel and it still exists today.

Dina: We traveled as much as we could. But these were not calm times. These were difficult times. My absorption took place during a period that was extremely difficult in Israel, on top of the physical difficulty in Hulata. We lived in hard conditions and we ate very poorly. But I was not bothered by it, because I had come out of the Holocaust with no appetite. Food did not interest me at all. What did interest me were the aesthetics of the food. To this day, I remember that we used to sit at the table and one of the members, whose nickname was Stalin, did not wash his hands thoroughly, and his hat served all purposes; it was a towel, protection from the sun and even some kind of decoration. He used to wipe his hands with his hat. And these dark drops would fall from his hands, and he would stretch his hand to take bread, and sometimes a drop would fall on the plate. This disturbed me more than anything else; I could not get used to the lack of attention to everyday hygiene.

Life was so difficult; I imagine that each person probably had been educated differently and grown up differently and become accustomed to the conditions as they were, but it disturbed me very much. Also, this partnership, this being together with people, was very strange to me. I was accustomed to it, because I was in the camp in Germany with the Polish women and it was very unpleasant. I am a very individual person. Also, to go to the Kibbutz' general assembly meetings, where I understood only a quarter of what was being said, was unpleasant.

Ezra: The idea of the Kibbutz, the togetherness of the Kibbutz.

Dina: The togetherness of the Kibbutz appealed to me because Bezalel was there. When we first met, he told me that he was a member of a Kibbutz. I knew that I would follow him to a Kibbutz. When I arrived in Israel, I wanted to go to a different Kibbutz and live my own life for a while, to feel on safer ground, and only then to marry. Not that I regretted it. But Hulata was probably a difficult place for an individual absorption. They did it better when a group of immigrants arrived. Then the immigrants worked half days, and dedicated the other half to studies. The idea of the Kibbutz has to be explained, not just experienced. You need to study in order to fully comprehend it. If they had given me lessons about Zionism and about understanding the Kibbutz, perhaps, through the brain, it would have also reached my feelings and my endearment. I was not prepared for this. But still, at the same time, there were so many beautiful things in the Kibbutz. I remember walking one morning on my way to work and seeing new seedlings, and I was so elated at the sight of a new tree seedling growing, not for myself, but for everyone. This was something I had never felt in my life. With no preparation and without all the years that, for example, Bezalel spent in Mahanot HaOlim, with the blue shirt; I had to accept all of it within several months in order to better cope with this difficult life.

Ezra: And everything that was happening throughout the country; we were approaching difficult times, November 1947; the declaration of the establishment of Israel. How did you feel?

Dina: I think it went over my head. From the personal standpoint, a change of this magnitude—getting married and living in a place I was not at all used to—it was like a completely different planet. The collective struggle towards independence probably went over my head because I did not recall my own big excitement. I remember, on the night we heard the declaration, we did not dance. Feelings are probably something that can be cultivated but also numbed. You cannot feel everything all at once, on so many different levels. There is a maximum amount that one can tolerate. I registered and felt more about things like not being part of the circle of fellows, than about the declaration of a State. These things influenced me much more than this big thing because it was as if this big thing belonged to everyone. Of course, I felt the happiness and the hope that we could get rid of the British. And there was also the concern of what might happen to the small family unit.

Ezra: When did your parents arrive?

Dina: My parents only arrived in 1948.

Ezra: Shootings began in the Galilee. You had already heard many shots. Did you have this sense of questioning the reason for arriving here?

Dina: I had this feeling that there I had been on my own, and had to deal with things by myself, whereas here, it was happening to everyone. It was not the same fear. I wanted to find peace, but this unsettlement was not only mine; it was also the collective unsettlement of the whole Kibbutz, of the entire Galilee, of the entire country. It did not frighten me at all; it never occurred to me that I could get killed there; after all I had gone through. I was most afraid that they would take Bezalel from the Kibbutz, because I knew that it would be difficult for me to cope on my own. I did not feel at home. This was not my home. As much as I wanted it to be, as much as Bezalel's friends were there, close by and wanting to help. Everyone had their own problems; it was a time of difficulty and stress. The people did not have any more strength. They had to send a quota of individuals to the army, and they started to dig bunkers and make preparations. In the meantime, my sister arrived at Kibbutz Ma'ayan Baruch, because my cousin, Izzi Lavie, was there. Once my sister had arrived, we waited for our parents. And I was on the Kibbutz and unable to help.

Ezra: How long had it been since you had seen your sister?

Dina: I left Germany at the end of 1945, and I saw her again a year or so after I came to Israel. She lived in Ma'ayan Baruch, and we did not meet often. We also corresponded the whole time with our parents. My brother stayed in Germany, and our parents arrived in 1948, during the war. My sister, in fact, also arrived during the war, with Aliyah Gimel.[62] And then there was a problem with our parents, because they arrived in Tel Aviv and received an apartment on the sixth floor of a building situated on the border between Jaffa and Tel Aviv. And this was exactly where the most severe shootings were taking place. They had no livelihood and nothing to live on. So Kibbutz Hulata agreed to give us four liras a month, to cover their rent, and my sister left the Kibbutz in order to help them.

We stayed in the Kibbutz. In the beginning of 1948, I already knew that I was pregnant. Bezalel stayed in the Kibbutz for the meantime; the war was at its peak; the conditions were far from being good.

There was some kind of general antagonism towards us; I do not know how else to call it. They slowly and surely pushed us toward leaving the Kibbutz. All of the other members

---

62 Aliyah Gimmel (gimmel is the third letter of the Hebrew alphabet) was the code name given to illegal immigration by Jews to Mandatory Palestine between the years 1945-1948.

were already settled. We had a neighbor who had a pipe organ, and mice entered inside it and ate it up, but they also got stuck inside the organ and died, and their stench was horrible. That year, there was a mouse infestation in the Galilee. And we could not stand the smell, so we left our room and went to live in a tent, and we were the only members who lived in a tent; none of the other members lived in a tent.

And in the tent, the mice entered but then left. In the concrete block, they only entered... Bezalel used to work at night, fishing, and the mice came to me, crawling in my hair; it was unbearable.

•

In those days, the emphasis in the Kibbutz was on the wellbeing of the collective and not on the wellbeing of the individual. Personal issues or personal requests had no place whatsoever. The boots, worn by the men who worked in fishing, only reached their knees, and I claimed that this was a shame, since the boots did not protect them, as the water entered from the top and stayed inside them. I thought that there was a need to change to higher boots, so they blamed me for showing too much concern for my husband. I told them that anywhere else, a woman who treated her husband well was worth twice as much, whereas here it was considered a deficiency, because one should not seek the wellbeing of the individual. For example, one man used to take a pillow with him to the fishing, so that he could take naps during times of rest. For some reason, this became the joke of the Kibbutz.

•

Dina: At a certain point, they transferred us to Kibbutz Tel Yossef. They were evacuating the pregnant women and children from Hulata. I still had a chance to see the tanks that were coming from the Syrian side in order to attack us. But a miracle happened, and they turned around and retreated. They were shot at, but these were only gunshots, so probably miracles did happen there.

We were transferred to Tel Yossef and, suddenly, a strange situation was created there, because we were all in exile. We lived together and became a very close group; I felt much better there than in Hulata. Perhaps this happened because all of us were strangers there, not just me. But time passed and we returned to Hulata. I worked again with the children and the feeling improved.

My Hebrew had also improved in the meantime; I could already read a bit. This was a different story now, because I cannot exist without a book, or something that will challenge me intellectually; I cannot live. Do you understand? I had been living in some sort of wasteland. Yedidiah helped me a great deal in this; he devoted a lot of time to teaching me and guiding me in what I could read.

The Birth of Nimrod

Nimrod, our first son, was born on September 10, 1948, at the end of a pregnancy that was accompanied by many health concerns. But the force of life was stronger than the concern. I wanted to connect to the Israeli experience of those days, and I wished very much to be strong. I did not feel enough of a *Sabra* yet, and suddenly I was pregnant. During my pregnancy, I continued to work with the group of six children I had taken care of in the Kibbutz. Nimrod's birth took place at the end of the ninth month of my pregnancy, in the maternity ward in Afula. A short while after the birth, the three of us returned to our room in the Kibbutz.

From Dina's conversation with Ezra:

Ezra: You traveled from Hulata in order to give birth?

Dina: The situation was still unsettled. I remember going from Hulata a few days earlier because the nurse said: let's go, as I am not sure we'll be able to go whenever we want to. This week I thought about the fact that I do not remember where Nimrod's *brit milla* (ritual circumcision) took place. I remember that we gave him three names and that my father was there, as well as Bezalel's father. When they asked about the child's name, Bezalel's father said Yossef after his father, my father said Shmuel after his father, and Bezalel said Nimrod. Thus he had three names—Yossef Shmuel Nimrod.

I did not like the way they treated children in the Kibbutz. The parents could not visit during certain hours. I wanted to see the child, and they said you can come here only from such and such hour. We could still hear sirens during the night, and I wanted to be by the child. There are things that look ridiculous now, but once it was a rule that you could not break; you could not come to the children's house just because you felt like it. There are specific hours that are your hours, when you can take the child and, until then, he belongs to the Kibbutz. Once, I came when we heard a siren, and they were infuriated with me for not trusting the caretakers enough. I said that I did trust them, but I wanted to see my child, and that is all; I wanted to be with him because I was scared and not because he was scared.

Leaving the Kibbutz and Returning to Ra'anana

Dina: We reached 1949, and I continued to be unhappy about staying in the Kibbutz. In general, I was a bit better, but I knew that I did not want to remain in the Kibbutz. Bezalel saw my suffering and wondered if the success of his life was worth all I was going through; whether it was the right price to pay. Because it was not just a day or two; I suffered the entire time I was there.

Ezra: Did you consider it together or apart? Did you speak about moving?

Dina: We talked with each other. Once, he said, "Suppose we leave, what shall we do? I do not have any training; I do not know how to live outside; I do not know what I will do; we have a child; we have to think about what we will do outside." I told him that I was willing to do whatever I could, and I did. When we left the Kibbutz and returned to Ra'anana, I worked in a kindergarten as an assistant to the kindergarten teacher.

Ezra: When did you leave?

Dina: We left at the end of 1949 or the beginning of 1950, I do not remember exactly. In the beginning, we lived in Ra'anana, together with Bezalel's parents. It was a two-story house that Avraham Freiman, Bezalel's father, had built. When half an apartment on the second floor became available, we moved in. Thus, his parents had the privilege of having their oldest grandson near them. It was probably not too difficult for me to convince Bezalel. Probably, he too was quite disappointed with the system in Hulata; he probably also wanted to study and knew that they would never send him from Hulata to study. It may have been a great mistake—the way they chose to absorb people—because, out of all the immigrants that came later, only one stayed. Hulata did not know, or the Kibbutzim did not know, how to absorb these people; they had no idea how to handle them. At a later point, I no longer had the feeling of being a foreigner or of not belonging; I simply did not wish to live there. And this was not easy, because we had no place to go. Bezalel left the Kibbutz first, in order to find work. I stayed behind, and the delegations began to arrive, one after the other, asking us not to leave, and where was I taking Bezalel? To the jungle outside. And what was he going to do out there? He had not been brought up like this; he would be miserable there. And this was true; there was a period in which he was miserable; nothing made him happy; it was difficult for him to adjust to life on the outside.

Ezra: Was he sad about leaving the Kibbutz?

Dina: He was sad because he felt he was not contributing his part
        in the greater mission. He felt that he was betraying some-
        thing. What his friends thought about him mattered a lot to
        him, and he was miserable because he could not go back to
        Hulata for visits; for an extended period of time, we did not
        travel. He felt like he was not acting correctly, that he was
        not doing right by himself. It was also hard because he was
        earning very little, and we wanted to sustain ourselves, and
        it was this sort of struggle between the wish to satisfy me
        and the desire to feel in total agreement with himself, and
        it did not work, and there were times when I said, "Let's
        go back. I'm not so happy here that it justifies you feeling
        so miserable." I saw his misery. The Galilee was not safe; it
        was not populated and every person who left weakened it.
        To this day, he feels that leaving the Galilee was an offence
        against something he was raised to believe in, yet he still left.

        My conscience was very unclean; I felt that I was to blame
        for his way becoming twisted; for something taking him
        away from his destined path. More than once, I thought that
        if Bezalel had married a girl whom he had known growing
        up, then their paths and their world views would have been
        similar. Because, for example, Carmela was there, and she
        had been his girlfriend before she got married. I thought
        to myself that this was a girl who really suited him better;
        that she would not have suffered or taken him out of his
        framework.

        However, I could not have been someone else; I did not
        wish to be; if you lose who you are, you are neither this nor
        that.

Bezalel

Dina: As soon as Bezalel began studying, the situation changed. Perhaps because Bezalel had to set a target for himself; he could not survive just for the sake of earning his living and going to concerts; he needed a purpose. In 1951, he began studying economics, and the country really needed economics back then. There was a need for rapid development, and everything was so fresh, he felt he could do something with it. He worked for a while in the Ministry of Education, and he already began to feel the action there. Because, together with Baruch Biran and Hadassah Benito, he opened the first intensive Hebrew schools for new immigrants. He also put together the team of teachers and coaches, and this started from nothing. It involved many trips around the country. He had this feeling of achievement, of not working just for his own benefit, which he simply could not do; that is how he was built.

Ezra: Did Bezalel maintain contact with the group of sailors and ship leaders during those years?

Dina: He had some contact, but nothing close.

Ezra: Do you recall the matter of the sailors' strike[63]?

Dina: Bezalel did not partake in it. I will tell you about Bezalel's character—he does not live in the past. When he was in Hulata, he contributed his part; he suffered for a few years

63 The 'Sailors' Strike' also called 'The Sailors' Revolt' is the name given to the tough professional struggle of Israeli seamen that began at the end of 1951. The strike erupted after the elections for the sailors' union were won by a nonpartisan list that sought better wages and working conditions and it was led by Nimrod Eshel, a former member of the Palyam. This, Israel's first strike, rocked the country and threatened to undermine faith in the new state's leaders and institutions.

because of leaving, but then he disconnected himself. He was in the Palyam, he was in the Palmach, and he did his share. As soon as he began his studies, his head pointed onward.

Ezra: How do you, as an immigrant, recall it?

Dina: I remember that period, and I remember the conversation we had. Bezalel said that the people who were in the Palyam at that time had to do certain things, and they did them with the highest measure of loyalty. Then, the country was established and the same people with different motivations and under different conditions acted according to how the moment dictated.

Based on his reply, you can understand what my claims were. My claims were that they had ruined my 'gods'; that they had shattered my tablets. Because I had icons. In Italy, I did not turn them into gods, but I did make heroes out of them. I turned them into people who did above and beyond their capabilities and withstood tests that were beyond imagination. Not that they did this on their own, the refugees helped them, themselves acting bravely after all of the hardships they endured; but it was initiated by them. And to take such a group of people and shatter all the illusions, this was very unpleasant for me, because you must always look up to something in life, strive for something. For me, they set an example as a group. And Bezalel was very practical. He said that they had done what they had done because it needed to be done, and now they were different people.

Ezra: Nimrod grew up; he carried these other two names. Were they written in his identity card?

Dina: No. only his grandfather, Bezalel's father, called him Yossef, Yossale. Meanwhile, Bezalel finished his studies and moved in the direction of industry and began to be very successful there. He really enjoyed working there, because it was vibrant, alive and breathing.

Ezra: He began his work at Koor?[64]

Dina: He worked at the Ministry of Education and he studied. He graduated from university in 1954 and began working at Koor several days after Hana was born.

Marek

During my sister Hanka's stay in Munich, she was busy organizing the reunion with my father and brother. They returned to Europe from Russia, where their complicated route had led them after their escape from Koszyce in the beginning of the war. It had been a long and challenging journey for both of them.

From their stories, we learned that one day, my brother and my father were added to a group of Jews that was led into the woods and there, instead of being murdered, were left to their own devices. My brother succeeded to keep my Father safe along the roads they were traveling, on foot or by car, for many weeks, into the depths of Russia. They reached Lwów and stayed there until the beginning

---

64 Koor Industries—Solel Boneh Construction, founded in 1924, by the Histadrut (the General Federation of Labor), created an industrial arm called Koor Industries, in 1944. Many of Koor's early employees were immigrants, who had escaped Europe. By 1958, Koor had grown to 25 plants with 6,000 employees. In 1971, Koor took over the government-owned trading company and renamed it Koortrade. This new subsidiary promoted Koor products in export markets and represented other manufacturers who could not afford to establish their own trade promotion groups.

of Operation Barbarossa, in June 1941.[65] Up until that time, my mother used to send to them food packages, as many as she could afford. Afterwards, my father was sent to Tashkent and Marek was sent to Gorky.[66] Later on, after a period of time, Marek managed to join my father in Tashkent, where he looked after all of Father's needs, until the end of the war. In Tashkent, Marek began to do business with the locals and was very successful, despite the fact that he had arrived empty-handed. This was also the place where he met his future wife, Sarah.

In Tashkent, my brother dealt, amongst other things, with purchasing fabric for men's clothes, an occupation that was relatively rare in the days following the liberation. He somehow succeeded, together with a Russian partner, to lay his hands on the expensive fabrics. By the time he returned to Germany, he had already earned a considerable amount of money through those business transactions. My brother had liked dressing smartly, since childhood. Later on, as a business owner in Canada, he used to wear a custom made suit, for one season only, and then send it to Bezalel. This way, Bezalel came to own the wardrobe of a "Polish nobleman."

While my father, my mother, and Hanka chose to follow me and immigrate to Israel, my brother decided to immigrate to Canada, since his wife, Sarah, was afraid of the shooting in *Eretz Yisrael*. In time, he became the owner of a hotel supply business and thrived over the years. He was one of the first people from the west to start

---

65 Operation Barbarossa was the code name for Nazi Germany's World War II invasion of the Soviet Union, which began on 22 June 1941. The operation was driven by Adolf Hitler's ideological desire to conquer Soviet territory as outlined in his 1925 manifesto *Mein Kampf*.

66 Gorky—The city Nizhny Novgorod, colloquially shortened to Nizhny. From 1932 to 1990, it was known as Gorky, after the writer Maxim Gorky, who was born there. The city is situated at the confluence of two of the most important rivers in its principality, the Volga and Oka Rivers.

doing business with China, at a time in which no one else dared to do it. Marek (who chose to be called Morris in Canada) and Sarah had two children—Feigi and Sami (Shmuel), who still live in Canada. We got to visit them several times.

From the perspective of his attitude towards the family, my brother changed. From a young man who loved entertainment and felt little responsibility for his sisters and his parents—as I perceived it as a child—he became a person who was highly responsible for others. The reality of our family splitting in two, in which he had to go through many difficulties in Russia while guarding his own life as well as our father's, caused him to mature quickly, and revealed new depths and qualities in him.

It gave me an opportunity to change the way I viewed my brother. I understood that he was, in fact, the one who saved my father by taking upon himself the responsibility of providing all of his needs and protecting him during those war years in Russia. He had also ensured my father's return to Europe through very complicated ways, until he was reunited with my mother and my sister. My relationship with my brother changed in a profound way and I learned to value him anew, as a man and as a brother. For years, Marek used to send food packages to Stefkova and to Janek in Poland, and supported our parents and us, as well. I loved to hear his war stories and his post-war tales whenever he came to visit us in Israel.

Hanka

When Hanka arrived in Israel, she joined Kibbutz Ma'ayan Baruch, where she met Yehuda Lewis, who was a veteran of the South Africa brigade. After a short period of courting, the two were married. After a while, Hanka and Yehuda decided to leave the Kibbutz, in order to help our parents, who lived in Tel Aviv, and to try and acclimate themselves to the country.

In the meantime, Tirtza was born and, approximately two years later, in 1951, Hanka had to undergo thyroid surgery. It was decided that the operation would take place in South Africa, where Yehuda's parents lived. On the night after the surgery, Hanka died in the hospital in her sleep, as a result of a hemorrhage. The American surgeon, who had gone there in order to teach these types of surgeries, wished to put an end to his life after he heard of her sudden death. Her death happened on the eve of Passover. First, we received notice that her surgery had been successful, and then we received a second notice announcing her death.

My beloved sister Hanka, my guide, my guardian angel, who had protected me throughout my childhood and the years of war, the best friend I ever had, died in a remote place and was buried in Cape Town. Her headstone was prepared out of natural stone. In 1974, I traveled with Bezalel to visit her grave.

Following Hanka's death, I went through an enormous crisis. I neither ate nor slept, which led to such health complications that I contracted tuberculosis.

In the Hospital

Ever since the war, my health had not been at its best and its condition had further worsened during my work on the Kibbutz. I now suffered from a low body temperature and coughing. A doctor I saw sent me for further tests in a hospital, where I was diagnosed with tuberculosis. I went through a difficult surgery, in which a large part of my left lung was removed (the operation was successful and years later, when I was x-rayed, I discovered to my great joy that my lung had grown back to its natural size). I was treated with antibiotics, which were already being used in those days and administered to those who suffered from tuberculosis.

•

From Dina's conversation with Ezra:

When I entered the hospital, Bezalel was studying, Nimrod was young and Bezalel's mother had broken her leg. So Nimrod had to be in the care of strangers, because there was no one to look after him. It was the most difficult time in Bezalel's life. He did not want to stop his studies, so he couldn't take care of the boy, who was left with a neighbor, and he couldn't come to visit me as often as he wanted, because he couldn't tear himself into so many pieces. He had to be a student, a worker, a father and the husband of a sick woman; it was not easy. But he did not stop his studies. I was in the hospital, in what is nowadays the Loewenstein Hospital but used to be a hospital for people with lung diseases. I was there for a year and a half; this was not a matter of a month or two.

•

My stay at Loewenstein Hospital in Ra'anana was interesting in many ways, because I met people whom I would never meet under different circumstances. I met young Yemenite women who had gotten married at a very young age, to older men. When these women arrived at the hospital to treat their tuberculosis, they were also given an opportunity to attend various courses for the development of women. They did not want to return to their homes, where their strict husbands awaited them.

We did not discuss our illnesses, but rather spent our time reading, writing letters and planning cultural events. We prepared plays for the Jewish holidays. I remember the Purim show with Esther Hamalka (Queen Esther) and the show for Shavuot with the characters of Ruth and Boaz. We presented Ruth as a young Yemenite woman and the young Yemenite, who stayed in our department, was the star of the show. It was her first performance in front of an audience. I remember this period as a rather comfortable one.

Professor Adler, the hospital manager, had been in charge of a hospital for people suffering from tuberculosis, in the Czech Republic, prior to his immigration to Israel. Adler treated these Yemenite women in a fatherly manner and helped them more than once to bridge the gaps that had been created between them and their families due to the education they had received in the hospital. He coordinated meetings with the husbands and explained to them that they had to treat their wives differently. The women had grown stronger in their status and the husbands had to understand and accept this development. Professor Adler regarded this as his mission and did all he could to help them in their expanding world.

I met there a young man from Iraq, who was handsome and extremely short tempered. The man had five sisters towards whom he directed his rage. They used to call him "grumpy Akram," the kind and intelligent young man who turned, at times, into a wild beast. Another fellow was an engineer by profession. We became good friends and he made things easier for me during this period. We read the same books and used to discuss them and argue about them. I was already experienced in summarizing the books I read, following my childhood with my sister Hanka, but for him, it was a whole new territory. He listened to my explanations and learned to summarize books in an explanatory manner. I remember Thomas Mann's excellent book, *The Magic Mountain*,[67] was one around which we held many debates.

Upon my return, I had to restore my relationship with Nimrod, whom I had seen only when he came to Lowenstein Hospital to visit with family members. Apparently, my mother-in-law, Shoshana Freiman, who was the head of WIZO (Women's International Zionist Organization) at the time, had preferred to tell people that I was hospitalized in a mental institution, rather than admit that I had been hospitalized for tuberculosis, a disease that was regarded as an infectious disease and had an extremely negative stigma in those days. My brother sent me money from his first profits, so that I could hire a cleaning lady. He knew that I had returned from hospital and that I needed help. After a period of recuperation, I returned to my work in the kindergarten in Ra'anana.

---

67 Thomas Mann, *The Magic Mountain*, 1924.

The Birth of Hana

In 1954, when Nimrod was six years old, Hana was born, and we named her after Hanka.

Hana Tells about It:

The doctors at the hospital for tuberculosis patients said to Dina, my mother, that it would be best if she did not get pregnant, because this would endanger her life. She had probably already contracted the disease before she returned from the war, and she spent an extended period of time in the hospital. But she insisted that she wanted a daughter and, indeed, she had one, but only after many agonies. During labor, she suffered from a severe hemorrhage, and I was born in a very difficult Caesarean section, after which Dina was hospitalized for several weeks.

In fact, I came home without a mother. This caused her a severe trauma. Father's mother, Grandma Shoshana, took care of me during the first weeks after my birth.

Nimrod received a baby sister, and it seemed that this was not to his liking at all, as his mother had stayed in the hospital again. A six-year-old child, who has a new sister in his life and no one giving him the full attention he needs.

The Family's Life

During my first years in Ra'anana, I was mainly involved in raising the children, Nimrod and Hana; in being constantly concerned that Bezalel had what he needed; and in maintaining the house on 18 Maccabi Street. After I recovered from tuberculosis and the Caesarean section, it took a few more good years until I had fully recovered my health and returned to being fully functional.

I loved our small and united family and we shared many experiences, especially on Saturdays and holidays, when Bezalel stayed at home.

Yehuda, Hanka's husband, returned from South Africa, together with young Tirtza. I took her as my protégé and thus, three mischievous children shared our house. Yehuda took her as often as he could. When she started going to school, she moved in with him.

We were also constantly in touch with my parents, who lived in Tel Aviv. My father worked as an ice cube distributor, in spite of his advanced age and in spite of having been offered a position as a rabbi in *Agudat Yisrael*. Shortly after his death, my mother moved nearby, to an apartment on 28 Maccabi Street.

During that period, we were at the center of the Israeli experience of creating a nation out of nothing. We experienced all the events of the first years of the country together, and Bezalel was always at the spearhead of the activities towards the establishment of the Israeli industry, which was still in its early stages. He was also at the front of the first efforts to establish Israeli exporting to the rest of the world. He traveled to many countries, and I remember that dozens of Hamat[68] employees used to always welcome him at the airport upon his return—business trips abroad were so rare at the

---

68 One of the first factories in Israel that specialized in processing iron and metals. The factory held a main position in the metal division of Koor Industries.

time. Bezalel also had the chance to meet with state leaders, who came to Israel to watch the Israeli miracle appearing out of nothing.

We experienced the big immigration waves of the early 50s, the times of the *tzena*,[69] the attacks of the *fedayeen*,[70] the Suez Crisis,[71] and the general developments of the economy and culture in the newborn Israel, rising like the phoenix from the ashes, after 2,000 years.

The years of war in Europe had toughened me to such an extent that I saw everything in a logical perspective, and was glad to be part of the Zionist work that overcame difficulties and had 'No More' engraved on its flag—to never return to the times of the Holocaust, when we had been defenseless.

---

69 Tzena—austerity. From 1949 to 1959, the state of Israel was, to varying extent, under a regime of austerity, during which rationing and similar measures were enforced.

70 Arab *fedayeen* are militants or guerrillas of a nationalist orientation, mainly from among the Palestinian people. In the mid-1950s, the *fedayeen* began mounting cross-border operations into Israel from Syria, Egypt and Jordan, sabotaging and killing Israeli citizens, especially at the border areas of the country.

71 The Suez Crisis, also named the Tripartite Aggression and the Kadesh Operation, was the invasion of the Sinai Desert in late 1956, by Israel, in order to stop the Fedayeen attack. This coincides with British and French forces invading Egypt in order to regain Western control of the Suez Canal and remove Egyptian President Gamal Abdel Nasser from power.

How I Became an English Teacher

After Nimrod had grown up and started high school and Hana was already attending the elementary school in Ra'anana, I began to set my sights on a profession—teaching English. It was a natural choice, since my mother had seen to it already, during the years of war, that we would all know English well.

In 1965, I started studying English, in order to become a qualified teacher. In 1966, at the end of my training, I flew to London for a three-month course. Hana, who was 11 years old, was sent to Kibbutz Messilot, to stay with the family of my cousin, Dov Ben-Ari.

I felt at home in London. I felt at ease from the very first moment. I stayed with a woman who rented rooms in her house, and enjoyed a warm welcome. I was given a spacious room, and when I returned one day with one kilogram of tomatoes, rather than with just one, the landlords thought that I was a millionaire…

I used to go out in the evenings with a friend named George, whom I had met in the language school. I enjoyed his company, and we went together to watch many plays. We used to buy standing tickets for the balcony, because these were the cheapest ones. I graduated the course with a diploma of excellence, returned home and started giving private lessons, helping students prepare for the matriculation examination in English.

I was fortunate to have students who wrote in our memory book that they had been privileged to learn English alongside etiquette. Some of my students joined the army a few months after their final exams, and some of those died in the different wars—may their memory be blessed. I had the opportunity to see them young, beautiful and full of dreams that were cut short. For many years, I stayed in touch with quite a large group of young English students; one of them eventually became an English teacher herself.

Nimrod

Nimrod and Hana were two completely different children. Nimrod was a sharp-witted child, who used to tell jokes and he never laughed while telling them. He had friends and I was happy to host them at our house after school. Nimrod loved sports and reading. He was a tough, beautiful child.

After Bezalel decided to send him to high school outside Ra'anana, Nimrod went to *Tichon Hadash* (The New High School) in Tel Aviv. Bezalel himself was studying at the Gymnasia Herzliya, in Tel Aviv at the time. Despite the distance, Nimrod liked school very much. During school days, Nimrod lived together with Tirtza and her father. They were in the same class and became good friends.

Nimrod joined the Navy. He did it, perhaps, to follow in the footsteps of his father, who had been in the Palyam, which became the foundation of the Israeli Navy, after the country was established. He served as a submarine sonar operator. During the time of his service, the Israeli Navy purchased from England an old submarine that had been manufactured in the forties. The submarine was upgraded in the dockyards in Portsmouth, England. The crew sailed to England to train with this submarine, whose name was changed to Dakar.[72] On its way back from England, the submarine and its crew vanished, without leaving any trace.

Many friends sat with us during the days and nights after it happened; dozens of them came to comfort us during those long and unbearable days, as the search for the submarine began. As time went by, more young men died in different wars and, naturally, people stopped coming. Also, we did not ask anything from anyone.

---

72 For further reading about the Dakar submarine—please see the appendix entitled, "The Submarine INS Dakar."

After Nimrod's disappearance, the flowers lost their scent. Their colour turned gray. It was a period that is extremely difficult to describe. In the years that followed, Bezalel blamed himself for the fact that Nimrod had followed in his footsteps. I took the stance that life must go on.

Hana spent the early years of her childhood with Nimrod. She was a happy and lively child. She had many girlfriends, and one of them was always close to her heart. They both treated us as if we were a queen and a king, and they were proud of us.

I was the one who told her that Nimrod was considered a missing person, and we argued about who would be the first to hug him when he returned. I did not turn the house into a graveyard and, therefore, we tried to deal with it as little as possible. Hana continued her piano lessons; and following my request, a good friend of mine took her to buy new boots.

After it happened, Hana chose to occupy both bedrooms—hers and Nimrod's. That way, her presence filled the house, and Nimrod's room did not stay tightly closed. Over the years, we used to talk about him as though he was present, as though he was still out there on a mission and had not yet returned from it. I felt that my task was to support everyone in the family.

My brother, as well, actively participated in this. He came from Canada, in order to be present at all the ceremonies. For years, he sent us money so that we would be able to travel around the world and would not sit at home mourning. While abroad, we were able to laugh a bit and remove from our shoulders the burden of waiting for an answer.

Over the years, relationships between the families of the missing submarine soldiers were formed and the joint ceremonies that took place briefly united the families.

Dakar was found, after 31 years of searching, exactly on the course where it was meant to be—opposite the shores of the Island of Crete. Over the years, it had been obvious that the State of Israel would not allow the mystery disappearance of the submarine to remain unsolved.

Hana studied in Ra'anana both in elementary school and in high school. Upon joining the army, she was assigned to Shalat[73] service in Kibbutz Tzuba, near Jerusalem, where she met Erez, who later became her husband.

The rest of the story, unfolding from this point onwards, I leave now in the hands of the beloved members of our small family to tell…

---

73 Shalat—an acronym for unpaid service—is one of the IDF's training options. The Shalat soldiers are regarded as reserve forces that are activated in times of emergency.

At our wedding

My parents, Yehiel Shlomo and Tonia Minzberg,
after their immigration to Israel in 1948

Bezalel and his parents,
Avraham and Shoshana Freiman

The agricultural colony of Ra'anana, 1947***

With Bezalel, Ra'anana

With Bezalel, Kibbutz
Hulata, 1948

During our time in the Kibbutz

Fishing in the Hula Lake, Kibbutz Hulata****

During the time in the Kibbutz

With Nimrod, 1955

With Bezalel

Bezalel

With (left to right): My sister Hanka, my father, Yehiel Shlomo, my mother, Tonia with young Tirtza and Bezalel with young Nimrod

The tombstone on Hanka's grave.

With Bezalel, Ra'anana

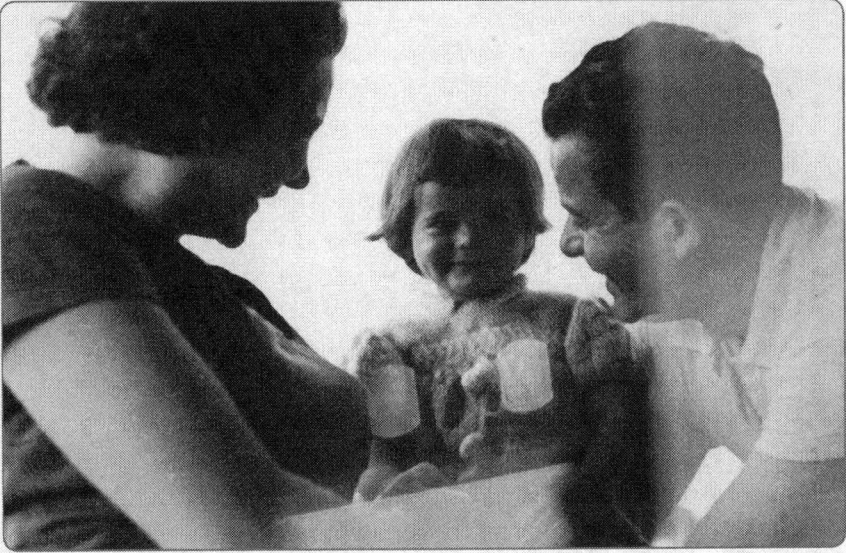

With Bezalel and young Hana

Tirtza, Nimrod and Hana

With one-year-old Hana, 1955

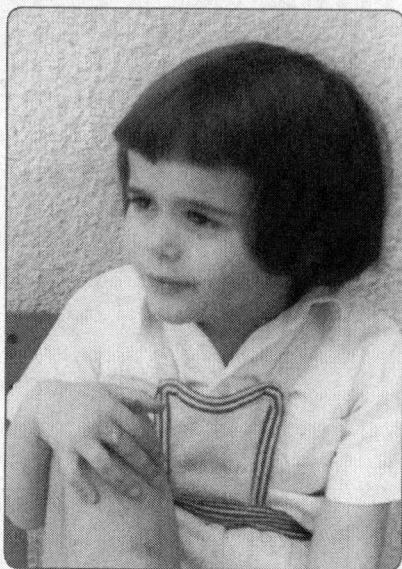

Hana, 1958

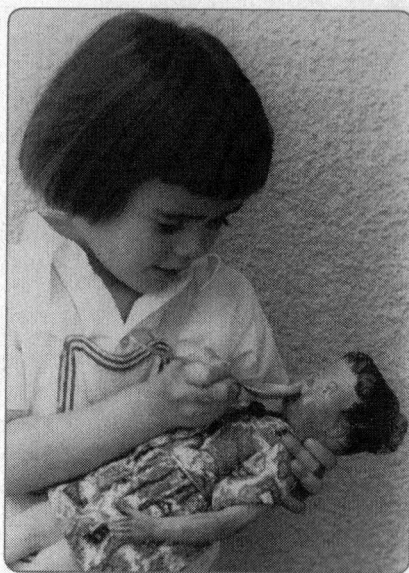

Hana and Nimrod, 1958

With Hana

Hana and Nimrod, 1958

Tirtza, Nimrod and Hana

Nimrod and Hana

Nimrod

Hana

Language Tuition Centre

L.T.C. SCHOOL OF ENGLISH
26-32 OXFORD STREET,
LONDON · W.1
(Recognised by the Ministry of Education)

This is to Certify that

Miss D. Drori

was awarded the DIPLOMA of this school

on the 26th August, 1966 **having completed the following course of instruction and attained the standard indicated below :—**

Subject :   English Language

Grade of Class   V

I = Beginners' Class	IV = Upper Intermediate
II = Elementary Class	V = Advanced (Stage 1)
III = Lower Intermediate	VI = Advanced (Stage II)

Tutor's assessment of competence in English :

Oral work   Very Good

Written work   Very Good

Comprehension   Very Good

Description of Course :   Fifteen Hours   weekly

Duration of Course: from   4.7.66.   to   26.8.66.

Subsidiary Subject(s) :

(a)   from   to

(b)   from   to

(c)   from   to

Principal

Head Teacher

Certificate of graduation from the English training course at the school of languages in London

At Sami's Bar Mitzvah with (left to right): Tirtza, Bezalel, Sami,
Sarah, Marek, Hanusha, Feigi, Hana, Rivi, Izzi, Orit

With Bezalel

Nimrod

Nimrod in the navy

Bezalel with the late prime-minister Yitzhak Rabin
in a visit to Koor Industries

Nimrod in the navy

INS submarine Dakar**

INS submarine Dakar**

Chapter Five

The Family Members
Tell about Dina

Hana Tells about Dina

Perhaps, I will begin by saying that each of Dina's stories and each of her famous sayings, and her special and unique wisdom that enriches those who come in contact with her, are all based on real-life events that personally happened to her during her lifetime. These stories and sayings have spread to much larger spheres than the sphere of our small family. Sometimes a workman comes to do something in Dina's house and leaves with a new insight about life. In our lives and through our teachings, we often spread those insights as well. Sometimes we will not hear back about it directly, but rather through someone who has adopted a part of Dina's life wisdom and, thus, it returns to us via some kind of an unseen grapevine. And if we tell Dina about it, in an attempt to give her something back, as a mark of appreciation, she usually looks at us with an expression of surprise, mixed with joy—almost like a young girl—and will often say, "Did I say that?"

Each of the stories she has told us carries a much deeper meaning— for her, to begin with—and then for us, the people who are close to her; and then, for many others and, perhaps, even for something greater that is correct in this life.

For example, the story about Danushka (Dina Shpigel-Mendlebaum, who lives in Haifa, who is today the great grandmother of many children)—the four-and-a-half-year-old girl who sat under the table in the house in Koszyce, during the autumn of 1942 and said to the rest of the family members that they would not be the ones to enjoy the coal they were about to buy, but rather the Germans (an utterance that saved the lives of the whole family). Over the years, this story has turned into a principle that is well grounded in our family: "listen to young children—they may know better than you what is about to happen. Do not cancel them out as if they do not know anything…"

Or the amazing story about the accidental meeting on the train to Warsaw with that young man who turned out to be the nephew of the girl whose Polish certificates Dina carried with her. What are the odds of something like this happening? And how did Dina know, in a split-second decision, to leave all of her sparse belongings behind and only look straight ahead? Hesitation of any kind could have cost her her life.

Is it not true for all of us and throughout our lives—to know when to leave things behind and move forward? What is the point in carrying our past with us, if we do not have a future?

And now to my perspective on Dina's life story:

When Dina first arrived in Ra'anana as a new immigrant, everyone she met thought she was a *goya*. She survived the war with the help of Polish certificates, and her face looked completely different, at the time, in comparison to the faces of the local young Israeli women. However, Dina picked up the Hebrew language very quickly, something that was very useful in her process of naturalization. After Dina had started to colour her hair blonde, we used to say, humorously in the family, that she is "a blonde with a dark past!"

Generally speaking, my grandmother objected to the marriage of her son with a new immigrant who had experienced the horrors of war. This was her position until she met my mother, and this meeting changed her viewpoint completely.

Dina returned from the war probably already carrying what later developed into tuberculosis. The sudden shock she suffered as a result of the sudden death of Hanka, her sister, had its impact on her immune system, which had, up until then, succeeded in enduring all the difficulties, and now collapsed. Hanka was a tremendous source of strength for Dina. After my brother was born, mother spent an extended period of time in the hospital. Already then, the doctors advised that in her condition, it would not be desirable for her to become pregnant again, as this could endanger her life, but Dina insisted that and wanted a daughter and she knew, by some sort of intuition, that she needed to have one—which is what happened.

Great agony accompanied my birth; Dina went through an extremely difficult Caesarean section. She was hospitalized immediately afterwards, as the result of a severe hemorrhage, and I was given over to the care of my Grandmother Shoshana, my father's mother. Life in the house revolved around my arrival—a new baby girl and a sister to her elder brother, who did not get to have his mother back home, together with the baby. This experience was painful for him, as a six-year-old child. It was an incredibly traumatic experience for my mother—staying in the hospital for a few weeks without her baby, until the doctors permitted her to return home.

At that time, we lived on 18 Maccabi Street in Ra'anana, in a house that Grandfather Avraham, my father's father, had built. It was a two-story house, and we shared the second floor with another family from Ra'anana, a childless couple. The floor had four rooms, two kitchens, two bathrooms and two separate toilets, which was rather unusual in those days. The division was such that they had the more elegant part, and we had the more modest part. Grandfather and grandmother lived on the ground floor.

My father was working in those days in Hamat Metal industries, starting in the accounting department and moving up the ladder until he became the manager of Hamat. Before that, he had studied economics and law, in the Tel Aviv branch of The Hebrew University. His specialty was in preparing contracts. At a later stage, he went to work at the Koor Concern, as the deputy director of the Metal Division. At the end of his professional career in Koor, he was the foreign trade comptroller. At the same time, he volunteered in the council of Ra'anana, dealing with issues of education and youth. Building youth centers for disadvantaged populations was at the core of his activity. As a former member of the HaMahanot HaOlim youth movement, encouraging different communities of new immigrants to move forward in their lives was important to him.

He had three motifs in his life: the first one was related to the State of Israel, its existence and its economic and social advancement. The second was the human aspect, which had in it integrity and justice—his main qualities. As a warmhearted person who showed interest in others, he used to conduct personal conversations with his employees and asked them how they felt at the end of the work day. It was important to him that they did not take work problems home with them. He used to mediate between people who quarreled, and he could do it because of his ability to see the truth and to be impartial. He was an arbitrator before the concept had even been invented. His love for Dina was the third main motif in his life and it included, as well, the value he held for her as a person, as a companion and as a mother. He used to consult with her about all the issues he dealt with—the ones that were of utmost importance. Her point of view was important to him because of her special wisdom, her broad scope and her cleverness. He, himself, had endless generosity towards our small family, and he was busy helping and promoting each one of us in the path we chose.

As a child, I felt that I had been born into the ideal family, with a very loving mother and father who radiated their love for each other. They used to always walk hand in hand, kissing each other in public.

My brother was a kind of role model for me. We played together with my cousin, Tirtza, and carried out many pranks in our youthful follies, along the entire length of Maccabi Street, which had ascents and descents that are fantastic for children's games. I remember well how we used to tie a wallet with a string and parade it on the street in front of passersby, while we hid in the bushes on the side of the road, pulling it away as a person would bend to pick it up.

The large swimming pool that used to be at the end of Maccabi Street was our playground for water games. Mother did not know how to swim and father tried to teach her during every vacation. At every opportunity, we had a chance to hear the famous story—of her drowning in the Wisla—as well as Dina's other water stories:

On one of Dina's and Irka's trips along the river, when they were ten years old, they jumped into the water and Dina found herself drowning. Someone, who happened to be there by chance, jumped into the water and saved her. The experience of sinking under the water caused a traumatic effect that lasted for many, many years. When Dina had to jump from the ship Shabtai Levinski into the sea and swim towards the beach, Bezalel, who knew about her fears, passed her on to a friend of his, Israel Wein, a Palyam member from Ra'anana, and told him, "Take this woman and throw her into the water."

On holidays, we traveled for vacation across the country. My mother's idea was that children need to sit in the sun, absorb its warmth and get stronger. Therefore, we often traveled with mother and grandmother to the beach in Herzliya. We sat there, Nimrod, Tirtza

[239]

and I, on the sand and in the water, sharing summer experiences of building castles in the sand and eating sweet watermelons.

When we went with father, it was usually a trip with a tent. We had a British tent from the Second World War. It was a military tent, made of thick canvas, and you needed heavy metal pegs to raise it up. I remember how long and tedious the process of building the tent was… by the time we had finished, it was nearly sundown, and we had to go back…

Father often flew overseas on business trips and, from time to time, mother would join him at the end and they would both continue, at their own expense, to many countries around the world. I have always valued my mother very much—her strength to move on, to progress, and to not remain in sorrow and sadness regarding things one cannot change; to accept reality, as difficult as it may be, as a platform for creating a joyful life, full of wellbeing.

The stories she told me, about how she used her intuition and common sense throughout her life, have greatly influenced me. I have always asked myself how I would have acted in her place. One of the examples of her way of thinking is taken from the years when existence was difficult:

This began when she was pregnant with Nimrod in Kibbutz Hulata. The moment arrived for receiving a maternity dress, and they gave her the dress of a big woman who loved to eat. The dress was not only huge on Mother, it also had a big oil stain that could not be removed by washing in the Kibbutz laundry room. For Mother, appearing in public in such a dress was an absolute disgrace. Later, we learned that even during her time in the labor camp in Germany, there had been someone who washed her clothes.

Years later, since appearances were vital to her, my mother wanted to buy herself a nice dress. She mentioned to Bezalel that she was going to look for a proper dress on the main street of Ra'anana.

Father reminded her of the poor economic situation we were in at that time. This remark ignited a strong resolve in her to look for a creative solution. That day she entered the Hollander dress shop, the only exclusive dress shop in Ra'anana in those days. During her pleasant and casual conversation with Mrs. Hollander, Dina discovered that a young member of the Hollander family was having difficulties with his English lessons. Dina was very glad to offer her help, once Mrs. Hollander asked her to teach him proper English.

This is how Dina began to teach English. The rumour spread quickly and she gained recognition in the town as an English teacher. In 1966, with my father's encouragement, she chose to travel to England to complete a concentrated course for English teaching. During her time there, she saw a great deal of theatre and even saw the famous World Cup football match between England and Germany, in which England won. So it happened that, following an offhand remark made by Bezalel concerning the economic situation in those days, and because of my mother's independent character, spirit and love for aesthetics, she became the most notable private English teacher in Ra'anana, coaching hundreds of children.

My appreciation for my mother's way of dealing with life's surprises has only grown over the years. The death of her sister presented an enormous difficulty. She named me after her. Her tremendous insistence on moving forward wisely, reappeared in all of its magnitude after the disappearance of the Dakar submarine, which was lost in the depths of the sea, together with my brother.

One of the things I somehow remember about my brother, Nimrod, is the enigmatic thing he always wrote in his notebooks: Nimrod Drori, 18 Maccabi Street, Ra'anana, Israel, the Solar System, the Milky Way, the Universe. Perhaps that was his way of expressing the bigger picture as he perceived it philosophically. I really loved this approach and adopted it later. Today, I think that Nimrod, in his humble way, knew that he was part of a much larger complex. I often saw him creating geometrical drawings—of ships, mainly. Perhaps this was due to the immigration genetics of our parents, or perhaps this was an early premonition of what was to happen.

As said before, as a girl, I thought that we were the ideal family and I often feared that something might happen to us. Later, when we were informed of the disappearance of the Dakar, it was a horrible time for us all and, especially then, during this period, I was amazed by the way my mother conducted herself. With all of the difficulties and the grief that engulfed us all, she had the strength to move forward. Her thoughts and her awareness were given to us, no less than to Nimrod and, in this manner she succeeded to not turn the house into a museum of memory and to allow life to continue despite the shadow of such massive loss.

During first few months, Father participated in the searches for the Dakar. He sailed with those who were searching, since he was a Navy man. It was a very difficult and noisy period in our house. I remember a large crowd of people surrounding us the entire time. At a certain point, Mother asked me about my piano lessons: "There is no reason for you to stop playing," she said.

The submarine was declared missing several months after its disappearance, and all of its crew members were reported missing in action. This broke our hearts. I heard my parents crying privately during the nights. At a particular stage, Dina decided that the crying needed to stop; she refused to wear black dresses, as was customary. Mourning mothers wore black dresses for at least a year. She refused to live according to the stereotype of the "mourning mother" and continued her life in as normal a way as possible.

I remember how she insisted that the three of us would travel abroad during the summer that followed the event. It was an organized trip to Europe that lasted several weeks. My parents met many people there, and we all became a united group. It was a joyful trip full of plazas, historical sites and breathtaking natural scenery. We returned from the journey a bit more strengthened.

Thus, upon our return to Israel, a new period began but bereavement continued to haunt our extended family. When we landed, we were informed that Orit, the daughter of my mother's cousin Izzy Lavie, and his wife, Rachel, had been killed in a car accident during her military service. Apart from Nimrod and Orit, who were killed in the same year, two more cousins were killed in the following years; both had been Air Force pilots: Ehud Ben-Ari, the son of Itzhak and Beatrice from Kibbutz Yakum, and Yehuda Ben-Ari, the son of Dov and Rachel from Kibbutz Messilot.

I joined the army in 1972 and wanted to go to Shalat. I had a friend named Amiram Kriger, who was a neighbor, a family friend and a good friend of Nimrod. He had completed his military service in the *gar'in* (core group) of HaMahanot HaOlim in the Nahal,[74] and suggested to me to go to Kibbutz Tzuba, where I would find other friends from Ra'anana. I agreed to try it.

I arrived at the Kibbutz, together with my parents. I was at the end of my hippie period. I particularly remember wearing clothes that were not to my mother's liking. Before we left, my mother said: "Why don't you braid your hair into plaits, in order to look tidier?" I arrived with plaits, an 18-year-old girl, to meet the Kibbutz secretary in her room. This is how we met Bracha, Erez' mother. A wonderful woman. I entered the room and saw her long plait, and I saw Erez' three sisters with their long plaits, too. The meeting between the two families was excellent and flowing. In fact, Bracha

---

74 Nahal—acronym of Noar Halutzi Lohem, lit. Fighting Pioneer Youth—refers to a paramilitary Israel Defense Forces program that combines military service and the establishment of agricultural settlements, often in peripheral areas. In later years, the program expanded to include volunteering and social welfare projects. Its groups of soldiers formed the core of the Nahal Infantry Brigade.

also turned out to be my commander on behalf of the Kibbutz, during the Shalat.

Later, Bracha and Ezra became very close friends of Dina and Bezalel. Dina and Bracha became soul mates.

Bracha said that she had forgotten to arrange a room in the cabin I had been assigned to and suggested that I stay in a different cabin—in Erez' room, since he was serving in the army and was not meant to return to the Kibbutz for a while. When I opened the door to Erez' room, I saw his stuff all over the place. What caught my eye in particular was a Hebrew-English dictionary that had fallen on the floor. Back then, I had not heard the stories that were told amongst friends about the Kibbutz' first son, whose name was Erez and who served in *Sayeret Matkal*.[75]

Several weeks later, I met Erez himself in the dining room when he came home for one of his leaves. We exchanged glances and, in one moment, everything started between us...

•

Erez adds to this:

About my meeting with Hana, I can only say that I did not know that she had stayed in my room for one night weeks before we met—I learned about it only a long time afterwards. During one of my leaves from the army, I saw a new girl entering the Kibbutz's dining room, with a brown coat and long hair; I looked into her

---

75 Sayeret Matkal—General Staff Reconnaissance Unit is a Special Forces unit of the IDF directly subordinate to Military Intelligence. Primarily a field intelligence-gathering unit specializing in special reconnaissance behind enemy lines, Sayeret Matkal is also tasked with counter-terrorism, hostage rescue, and foreign espionage. Modeled after the British Army's SAS, from which it took the motto, "Who Dares, Wins," the unit's existence was initially kept top-secret.

black eyes and something in me knew that this was it. To this day, I don't know how I knew that I knew.

•

My parents stood by me the whole way, with openness, trying to understand, with full support and with consideration, also of the things they did not always understand.

In 1974, when Erez and I studied the new ways of the Emin group in England, Dina came to visit and to check that everything was alright. She participated in a few Emin meetings and wrote back to Bezalel and Erez' parents in Israel that everything was alright with "this thing."

In 1977, we returned to Israel and my mother organized the first Emin meeting in Israel for us. The meeting took place in my late grandmother's Tonia's apartment on 28 Maccabi Street in Ra'anana, where we were living at the time. A few years later, Dina and Bezalel joined a special group that we opened in the Emin for older members.

Ten years later, when we helped to establish Ma'ale Zvia—a Jewish-Israeli settlement, in the way of the Emin, in the Lower Galilee—my parents became inspired by this modern Zionist settlement and were filled with a wish to help its activities. They donated to the establishment of a research room that was named after my brother Nimrod, to the successful regional school that was established there, to the Little Marquise playground and towards the building of the Stream of Seven Colors that runs through the center of the village.

Erez Tells about Dina

It seems important to me to give this amazing weave of Dina's stories a bigger historical perspective, in order to understand at least part of their true value.

From an historical standpoint, Dina lived during an incredible crucible of events. She lived for three years under the Nazi regime in the Polish town of Koszyce. She was in Warsaw during the Warsaw Ghetto Uprising and the Polish Uprising. She was captured and sent to a forced labor camp in Germany, where she experienced the liberation of the camp by the American armed forces.

She took an active part in organizing the immigration to Israel, prior to the Israeli War of Independence. She participated as "a regular terrorist" in the blowing up of a British deportation ship. She took part in the very harsh, idealistic Kibbutz undertaking and experienced the War of Independence directly, as a young mother, living on the border of Syria. She also experienced the eight wars that followed. She became a bereaved mother following one of the Israeli military's biggest disasters—the loss of the submarine Dakar; she accompanied Bezalel throughout the road of establishing the Israeli industry and bringing it from its infancy to the stage in which it thrived; and she was a private English tutor who was famous in her own right. In all of these crossroads, Dina remained Dina, and her stories in this book emphasize it from so many different angles.

One of the significant historical crossroads she personally experienced was the time of the Polish Uprising. The agreement between the Red Army and the Polish underground was that the underground would commence the uprising at the same time in which the Red Army would invade the town. As agreed, the Poles initiated the uprising, with great success in the first few days—but the Russians stayed put across the Wisla River for nine whole weeks, until the German army had practically annihilated most members of the underground; only then the Russians began to bomb Warsaw for three more weeks. During the uprising, Dina was in Warsaw by herself, holding a fake Polish certificate. The citizens of the city found themselves in the middle of a crossfire between three armies— the Polish underground, the Germans and the Russians. At the end of the Polish Uprising, Dina was captured and transported, by the Germans, to a forced labor camp in Germany.

Today, we know that, at that time, Hitler gave the order to demolish Warsaw altogether, to annihilate its citizens methodically and to create a lake where the city once stood. The SS followed this plan thouroughly, with more enthusiasm than they showed in fighting the Polish Underground.

One of the smaller yet more significant things that touched my heart happened when we once looked together at the photographs in the family album. One of the photos is of the young woman who said to Dina at the time: "The day they burnt down the Warsaw ghetto was the happiest day of my life." Why did she keep this photograph in the album? Dina succeeded in keeping these photographs throughout the war years and the time of immigration, perhaps in order to send a message to that girl: "Look where I am now!"

And something else that relates to a different crossroads: how come a Jewish-Polish girl who grew up in a small town in the southern part of Poland knew English; a fact that saved her during the liberation from the forced labor camp, enabled her to find work after the war and, later on, served as a source of income… I believe that Tonia, Dina's mother, who had planned to move the family to the United States prior the war, had some kind of instinct that foretold the future and guarded her daughter along her journey.

I recognize this instinct well, both in Dina and in Hana. It probably runs like a leitmotif in the women of the family. It seems to me that Mey-Or, our granddaughter, has it as well…

[247]

But back to the beginning: I first met Dina when Hana invited me to their house; this was in the spring of 1973. Throughout the years, Dina has offered different "life lessons" to me. I was young, shy and quiet. One morning, I remained alone with Dina during breakfast. Sitting across from Dina, I noticed that she was not uttering a word. After a long while, I decided to ask Dina if she was feeling well. She replied by saying to me, "I only wanted you to taste what it feels like to sit across from you and not hear even one word from you."

One of her qualities, which is not shared by many, is her directness. She would share her thoughts with you regarding any issue and matter in the clearest and most direct way and without any hidden insinuations. She does not say something she does not mean, and she does not hint at something that can be spoken aloud directly. The lesson I took from her in this was that sometimes you have to be direct, and at times even blunt, and to express exactly what you see. In our family, we call this quality "Koszyce!" I recall a family story about how, many years ago, in one of the shops in Ra'anana, they asked Dina to show her identity card. She looked at the vendor, shocked by how her very being was not sufficient evidence for who and what she was.

Another insight, a vital one, with which Dina endowed us through-out our years of acquaintance, is to not let your feelings be the sole thing that manages you, but rather to allow your thoughts and emotions to balance each other. This aspect has expressed itself clearly in her way of life and in light of all the crises that life presented her with. When one looks at her ways of coping, anger or insult exist only superficially and, beyond that level, they have no control over her choices; she would never empower them. And indeed, the life situations in which she found herself as a child and as an adult have demanded a complex coping at every level—both emotionally and mentally.

Dina has always known how to move forward. I adopted this principle into my life and into the life of our family.

In the numerous conversations we held over the years, and especially after Hana and I chose the Emin's spiritual way of life, I became acquainted with Dina's religious outlook. She never embraces things as they are, but continues her path to search for the truth. She does not search for a particular belief, not because her father had been a rabbi or because religion does not exist. For Dina, the godly aspect has to prove its existence in a unique and personal way, and as long as she does not have evidence that settles her mind, she is not committed to believing in this or that existence.

I find it necessary to mention that, based on my acquaintance with Bezalel and Dina, Bezalel's promotions through all of his various positions and his relationships with the people who held central positions in the leadership of the country in those days, could not have been made possible without the support, wisdom and encouragement of Dina. Dina always stood by him, for him and as part of the national effort to create a country out of nothing.

Today, many years after the disappearance of the submarine Dakar and after the death of Bezalel, to whom she was deeply connected, perhaps something has begun to change in her in terms of acknowledging the immortality of the soul. She started to speak about essences that were built in our world and that are part of a different existence. We understood this issue via an incident that took place eight years after Bezalel's death. Dina decided then that it was time to replace their double bed. We bought a new bed, yet the following day she called to cancel the order. When we asked why, she replied: "I realized that Bezalel will not have a place to be in."

To hear something of this nature from such a balanced and logical woman like Dina; that she dreamt or heard her husband telling her,

"Where will I be if you replace the bed?" says a great deal about her ability and her openness to change in any situation and at any age. Recently, Dina told us that she hears Bezalel's voice and that she consults with him. She also speaks with her sister regarding substantive matters in her life, incorporating the rationalism that has characterized her with the world of hidden intuition.

Another circle was completed a few months ago, when Hana and I were invited to a ceremony in the Naval Army Base in Haifa, in which one of our family members was appointed to a senior position in the submarine flotilla. In his speech, he mentioned how the decision to join the submarine's unit had been born out of looking at Nimrod Drori's picture, which had always been in his bedroom, ever since he was very young. This was a very moving moment!

In conclusion, I would say that I have known Dina as a Polish queen. I respect her as a unique human being, who experienced the biggest war in the world, survived it and moved on. For over four decades of acquaintance and, in fact, from the first day I joined their family, Dina and Bezalel never ceased to support us in every possible way. Even though we chose a new, unknown and at times not accepted spiritual path, they always stood by our side. And, for this, I shall always be grateful to them and to their way.

I must say that I could not have wished for myself a mother-in-law better than Dina!!!

Nimi Tells about Dina

My first memory of my grandmother is to do with tastes and smells of the food she used to prepare in my childhood—the smell of the fresh tomato puree she would make, which I would eat with a teaspoon every day after kindergarten, and the sight and smell of the many cakes she baked. I remember asking Mother why she did not bake cakes the way Dina did, and she said that one could only find that flour in grandmother's grocery store. That story lasted for a few good months…

We call Grandmother by her first name, both my parents and I. This has been our custom throughout the years and calling this amazing woman grandmother does not suit her way and her personality.

She taught me English, and when we watched movies together, she used to answer my questions about the narrative. We did my home-work together. She once told about how one of her students gave her money at the end of the lesson, a crumpled bill he kept in his pocket. She said to him, "You will go home, iron the note and give it back to me in an envelope next week." This represents Dina to me; not only from the standpoint of aesthetics but also from the command-ing respect. "So it will have face," as she used to say, and not in the superficial meaning of the word! Everything you do needs to be respectful. This way, you become respectful in your own eyes and in the eyes of others. She would never wear a bathrobe, even when home alone. Mother once told me that after Nimrod's *shiv'ah* (seven days of mourning after the death of a family member), she dressed up, put her makeup on and went downtown. She never paid attention to others' criticism, because she always felt very confident about what was the right thing to do.

This ties in with a key story from the war. Just before the separation of the two sisters, Hanka told her, "What you need to remember is that no matter what you will go through in your life, after it's over, you are the one who will have to face yourself and look at yourself in the mirror." The most amazing thing is that this was something that was said by a twenty-year-old girl to a seventeen-year-old girl.

Another story I recall is that, during the period in which they were looking for the lost submarine, and everything was dark and gloomy, she looked in the mirror and said, "When I will feel happy again and able to laugh, I will permit myself to do it," and so she did.

Throughout my early childhood, we used to draw together. My grandfather and my grandmother took me for visits to various museums. I remember the blue colours in Chagall's and Monet's paintings. Upon our return home, we spread out papers and, together, Dina and I tried to paint like them. Hours upon hours of experiences with films, songs, language and drawing with her, were fundamental to my growing up.

Her serious approach toward me, the child, was evident. She valued my thoughts as a child and responded with sentences and conversations that showed her respect to young and old alike: "The fact that someone is older than you means nothing apart from the fact that he or she has had time to eat more potatoes than you have," she used to say to me.

Grandfather Bezalel was very happy with the close relationship I had with Dina. Since he worked and was often away from home, he used to appreciate the fact that I stayed in their house. I remember one day, when I was singing in one of the rooms in their apartment. They called me to the living room and asked me if I knew who had been singing, because my singing sounded to them better than what they expected from me at that time.

Bearing the name of my dear uncle, Nimrod, who was on the missing submarine, Dakar, always meant a connection and a sign of family pedigree for me. It is a name my mother loves. But I never felt the weight of the name upon my shoulders; its meaning for all of us is full of love and much respect. Dina knows well how to separate things. She insists on not burdening others with the meaning of my name. When I was born, she respected my mother's wish to commemorate the name of her brother, in spite of the pain involved. She had the ability to see in the new life that had arrived with me, the power of the spirit.

She listened to her inner knowing about his death; understood the meaning of the difficult things and chose to continue living. This strength to keep going is enormous; not from denial but rather from an upfront decision. She, who went through the horrors of the Second World War, found herself coping like other bereaving families upon the death of their sons and daughters, the young soldiers. She encountered people who had experienced bereavement and war amongst the families of her students and intimately felt their pain.

She always said, "If you are not true to yourself, you are not genuine... when a person starts lying to himself, that is the end." Dina will not lie or pretend she is something she is not, to herself or to others. She needs to feel real, in order to live a true and honourable life.

Reading was never one of my hobbies, ever since I was a child, but with Dina's help, I experienced, and still do, the contents of the books she talks about with such excitement. In every meeting with her, she would talk about the contents of books she had just read, or films she had just seen, in such a lively manner that literature came to occupy its place in my life, and I enjoy it very much.

I remember a sentence she used to say to us: "Never be mean when it comes to nickels and dimes." Money received its proper and respectful place, but the main thing was keeping it in proportion. Do not bargain with anyone about small change, because the person who bargains actually becomes mean and narrow-minded.

There is always the need to pay a working person in a way that shows respect; the man needs to know that he earned his wages in an honest way, and he needs to be rewarded generously.

The same approach was expressed in the generosity she showed towards causes that seemed worthy to her. One personal example out of many others, is her and my grandfather's support for my music studies over the years. They never gave me the feeling that I owed them something in return for their generosity.

For me, the two couples—both sets of my parents' parents—set exceptional examples of couple life and of mutual respect, which can pulsate between a couple living together. Gentleness and romance were also part of their guiding principles. Bezalel always used to say with his special smile, "Dina is the family commander..."

In fact, Dina has been telling stories all her life; key stories that have a message and a moral, so that we can all take with us, out of her life experience and her observation of people, provisions for our own journey. Her conscious decision to tell short stories that have a moral that she gathers out of her wisdom makes her stories tangible, available and inviting.

Gali Writes about Dina

Dina is like a sun shining in May
Even if it's on a wintry day,
She sends directed rays of light
To encourage growth, to do well, to clarify every might.

She discovers and transforms her endless information
Sharing, telling fascinating stories, seasoned
with special humourous generation;
With life-changing advice full of common sense
A path is opened towards something new and possible for all else.

A meeting, a glance, a smile
A little saying of Dina, worth a long while
Advancement even when at strife
Is really significant for every life.

The privilege and opportunity to meet a lady like you is so great
The contribution and the possible change you carry
without doubts or regrets
They give room and hope for humanity
To live a life of dignity and sanity.

Tirtza Writes about Dina

Aunt Dina, my mother's sister, a mother I hardly knew. I was privileged to receive from my mother two and a half years of warmth and love that charged me for many years. All the rest I came to know bit by bit through Aunt Dina's loving eyes. She told me many stories about our Hanka, about her inner and outer beauty; about her endless curiosity, about her great wisdom and her incredible knowledge of survival.

Dina raised me as her child, immediately after I lost my mother. I lived in her house for a year, together with Nimrod, my cousin, who was like a brother to me. Over the years, I became more and more amazed at the strength she had, to look after Nimrod and myself while mourning Hanka's death; Hanka, who was a sister, a mother, a friend and mentor to her. Bezalel always stood by Dina in order to assist and to encourage her.

Dina is a wonderful aunt and an extraordinary woman, who is a source of inspiration for me. I always feel the magical connection between us and, with her help, I continue to discover more and more aspects of my mother, Hanka, whose light shone, shines and will continue to shine over my life.

A Dedication to Dina on her Ninetieth Birthday

The word 'impossible' does not appear in Dina's dictionary

You are here with us after ninety years and you look like a queen—It may sound impossible, yet it is true.

You came out of a small Polish town, where a horse and carriage were the means of transportation, and you are here with us in this age of space and internet—It may sound impossible, yet it is true.

You said no to thousands of years' tradition and have stuck to your ideas from an early age, and you continue to do so—It may sound impossible, yet it is true.

You survived humanity's biggest war ever, and you were only a young woman, by yourself—It may sound impossible, yet it is true.

You found your entire family alive after the war—It may sound impossible, yet it is true.

From all the young men in the country, you specifically found Bezalel in Italy, and he brought you with an immigrants' ship to Israel—It may sound impossible, yet it is true

You helped to explode a British deportation ship without any prior training—It may sound impossible, yet it is true.

You slipped away from the eyes of the British Military on the way to Atlit—It may sound impossible, yet it is true.

Your ideals brought you to a Kibbutz, and you had the strength to leave it and begin a whole new life—It may sound impossible, yet it is true.

You lost your beloved sister, Hanka, and succeeded to move on in spite of this, while offering your love to her daughter, Tirtza—It may sound impossible, yet it is true.

You gave birth to Hana in spite of all the doctors' advice and against all odds, and you both survived—It may sound impossible, yet it is true.

You lost your son, Nimrod, and yet knew how to go on living for yourself and for the sake of the whole family—It may sound impossible, yet it is true.

You supported Bezalel in all that he did for the country and for the family—throughout the years and with great love—It may sound impossible, yet it is true.

You found a new profession for yourself and reinvented yourself as an English teacher, and were the best in Ra'anana—It may sound impossible, yet it is true.

Your daughter and your son-in-law joined a new way of life, and you knew how to continue to support them in spite of everything—It may sound impossible, yet it is true.

You prepared thousands of liters of apples' puree for your only grandchild and refused giving up any possibility to continue to support and believe in his dream—It may sound impossible, yet it is true.

You knew when to move to a senior citizen's home and to give up the beloved home in Ra'anana—It may sound impossible, yet it is true.

You knew how to support Bezalel throughout his illness—It may sound impossible, yet it is true.

You have continued alone for the last decade, since Bezalel moved on to a better world, and you still go on—It may sound impossible, yet it is true.

You continued to support Nimi and Gali the whole time, and you created a unique relationship with your first great-granddaughter,

Mey-Or, in spite of the age difference—It may sound impossible, yet it is true

You are ninety and still teach us about life, but with all that has been written so far—it does seem very possible and indeed it is true.

So, it is true—Impossible does not appear in Dina's dictionary— and we thank this fact every single day.

With much appreciation and with much love,
Hana and Erez

With Hana at her wedding,
Kibbutz Tzuba, 1975

Erez and Hana, at their wedding,
Kibbutz Tzuba, 1975

With Hana, Bezalel and young Nimi

With Bracha and Nimi at Nimi's Bar Mitzvah celebration

With Bezalel and Ezra at Nimi's Bar Mitzvah celebration

With Bezalel and Nimi

Erez, Hana and Nimi

Ezra and Bracha Grinboim

With Nimi

With Erez

With Mey-Or

With Hana

Nimi in the Opera

With Hana, Erez, Nimi, Gali and Mey-Or

Closing Contemplations

From Dina's conversation with Ezra:

Ezra: As we draw to an end, I want to ask you, Dina, now that we have sat together and you have told me your story, how would you like to conclude? And how do you feel now about this country?

Dina: I can say that I tie it, in a sense, to my love for Bezalel; and as I was never disappointed in my love for him, I feel the same about this country. I feel that I fell in love with the country from the moment I arrived. I do not know how to explain falling in love with a country—whether it is to do with the landscapes, or the smells, or the sights, or the people, but I fell in love with the country from the moment I disembarked from the ship. This love has accompanied me my entire life, and when I travel, I am impressed all over again. I mean, my love for the country has not weakened. And with this I conclude—I hold many hopes that such a love cannot be false; it must include in it something very, very intense and real, and I believe it will justify itself in the end.

Ezra: Yigal Alon said that love that needs explaining is not love. This is the country, and it is ours. Thank you very much, Dina.

Dina: Thank you very much.

Points of Light

Now, having reached the age of ninety and even beyond, I feel that I have lived a full life, and perhaps a few lifetimes within the life of one person. I am trying, as I have always done, to pass from my life experience to those who are closest to me; to Tirtza, the daughter of my sister, to her husband, Avi, and to their children; to my daughter Hana, to my son-in-law, Erez, to my grandson, Nimrod, to his wife Gali, and even to young Mey-Or.

Yes, five years ago, our family received a lovely gift—my great-grand-daughter, Mey-Or. The light she shines around her brings with it an indescribable joy. In spite of everything I have gone through, I feel rewarded by having such a family and by the fact that at the end of the chain is this ray of light—Mey-Or.

I am very proud of my grandson, Nimi, and of his success as an opera singer. From time to time, our small and united family sits together in my apartment at the senior citizens' home, and we watch short films from his performances. I am speechless, and in spite of the thousands of books I have read in my life, I have no words to describe the feeling of elation it gives me.

Every night I think about the blessed life I lived, together with Bezalel, and I give thanks to the fact that I had a chance to be in his company most of my life. Even though he passed away over ten years ago, I still consult with him, from time to time, regarding vital matters and update him on what is happening now.

And once in a while, when I am in my bed and wait for sleep to arrive, I feel a light nudge in my back and hear Hanka whispering to me, "Move over a bit and give me some room."

And I recall something funny:

They say that when Polish women burst out laughing, they roll with the laughter that comes out, surprisingly so, from their belly—something rather screechy. And I have always had a restrained laughter; I tend to smile a lot and avoid wild laughter. In my youth, I used to stand for hours in front of the mirror in order to mimic rolling laughs, but never succeeded. It is probably something one is born with.

On the occasion when my beloved and dear ones celebrated with me my ninetieth birthday, they all said that I look fantastic and have not changed a bit. Only my laughter has changed over the years... It has become less inhibited, and there are times when I roll with laughter. And I have, together with my daughter Hana, some completely uncontrollable fits of laughter. And when I look at her from the side, I tell myself how proud and lucky I am.

With Mey-Or

Appendixes

The Jewish Community in Koszyce

Koszyce is a town in the region of Kielce in the county of Pińczów in Poland. It lies on the banks of the river Szczerniawa. Koszyce used to be a regional center for craftsmen, and it was known for its textile processing. The local trade of wheat was developed as well.

Until the year 1862, Jews were forbidden to settle in Koszyce, because it was an ecclesiastical town. However, in 1827, 24 Jewish traders who used to arrive only for market days, settled in the town. As a result of their trade relations with the local community, they managed to rent houses and to remain in the place as guests for short periods of time, to begin with, and later as residents. By the end of the 19th century, the number of Jews had increased significantly, and by 1897, reached 366. The Jews of Koszyce earned their living from small trade and from handicrafts, especially tailoring, cobbling and carpentry. Some of them opened bakeries. Some of the traders had shops that sold haberdashery and textiles. There were many peddlers amongst the Jews of Koszyce, and they offered their merchandise in the nearby villages. Amongst the well-to-do Jews, there were a few wholesale traders of wheat.

In 1921, the number of Jews in Koszyce was 678, and they were 46% of the population. Even during the period of time between the two world wars, the Jews maintained their traditional occupations, but the economic stagnation and the heavy taxes that the government introduced in relation to Jews worsened their situation. During the economic crisis in the 30s, their status deteriorated even further. With it came the anti-Semitic propaganda that called for a ban on the Jewish trade and craftsmanship; propaganda that in most places in Poland was boisterous and succeeded in achieving its target, but in Koszyce took on a milder expression.

In the latter part of the 19th century, the Jews in Koszyce were already organized as a community. They had a synagogue (The Great Synagogue per the locals), a few smaller synagogues (*shtiebels*) that belonged to the Hassidim, and a cemetery; and the town had its own rabbi. The Great Synagogue was burnt down in a fire in 1927 and was never restored as a result of the economic crisis. From that time on, the Jews of Koszyce had to conduct their public prayers in private homes or in the *shtiebels* of the Hassidim, whose number grew after the fire.

In 1926, the Jews established a charity fund that eased a bit the distress caused by the lack of livelihood. The Jewish youth of Koszyce, and especially the members of the youth movements, actively participated in establishing the fund and even used to keep their savings in it in order to support it. The fund served to finance their professional training in the preparations towards the immigration to Israel.

During the period between the two world wars, the community life was highly influenced by the lively Zionist activity that went on in Koszyce. The community's committee collected donations for the Zionist funds, especially for the Jewish National Fund. At that time, a public library opened up and served as a place of gathering for Zionist conventions and community meetings. The youth as well used to meet there.

At the beginning of World War II, and as of September 5, 1939, the rule over Koszyce, and likewise in the whole county of Pińczów, was in the hands of the German military government. Already in the first days of the occupation, cases of abusing Jews took place. The soldiers demanded that the community rabbi supply them with a list of all Jewish inhabitants, and then gathered them in the market square and introduced them to threats. On this occasion, they warned them that any Jew who would dare to break any of their regulations, whether a small one or a big one, would be sentenced to death.

The Germans changed the former geographical division and annexed Koszyce to the county of Miechów, as part of the region of Krakow. In the first few weeks after the occupation, many Jewish refugees fled from the Krakow region into the county and into Koszyce. Many of the Jews from Koszyce fled to the east, to areas that were under Soviet rule, and their place was taken by the refugees.

At the end of 1939, the Jewish population in Koszyce reached around one thousand people, most of whom were refugees.

The Germans appointed a *Judenrat* and imposed on him to provide them with forced labor workers. Every day, the *Judenrat* provided a quota of forced labor workers who did not receive payment. The first decrees imposed on the Jews included the obligation to wear a yellow patch that was later replaced by a white armband with the Star of David on it; a prohibition from walking on the pavements; and also financial "donations." The Germans threatened that if the "donations" were not received on time, Jews would be executed. The Germans also confiscated the properties of the Jews. From time to time, the Gestapo would come and search for valuables in the houses of the Jews.

In 1940, the Jews were evacuated from their homes and herded onto one street; the *Judenrat* had to house the refugees in this small ghetto. In May 1941, the *Judenrat* opened a public kitchen for the sake of the refugees who had arrived in Koszyce empty-handed, hungry and tortured. This kitchen offered 120 meals on a daily basis.

The *Judenrat* sustained the kitchen with the help of aid money that came from the Juedische Soziale Selbsthilfe (JSS), a Jewish mutual aid organization from Krakow.

At the end of August, beginning of September 1942, all the Jews from Miechów County, including the Jews from Koszyce, were taken to a transfer camp in Salonika. The camp was built on a fenced-in meadow, under the open sky, and near a railway station. Thousands of Jews were held there with no food or water. The Germans conducted a screening, separating out 1,500 young and healthy men, with Jews from Koszyce amongst them. They were all transferred to a labor camp in Prokocim, in the outskirts of Krakow. The Germans murdered the sick and the elderly in the camp, and the others were transported by train to the concentration camp, Belzec.

A few dozen Jews stayed on in Koszyce and worked in sorting the possessions of the deportees. Then, on November 6, 1942, they were transferred to the Miechów ghetto, together with the remaining Jews from the Wolbrom and Nowe Brzesko ghettos. On November 7, 1942, all of the inhabitants of this ghetto were taken to Chodow Forest and shot to death.

The county's gendarmes and the Gestapo suspected that more Jews were hiding in bunkers in Koszyce and initiated a search. On November 12, 1942, they discovered seven Jews, took them to the Jewish cemetery and shot them to death. A few days later, ten more Jews from Koszyce who had been hiding in the village Milkowice were caught. They too were shot by the gendarmes and buried in the field. Only very few of the Jews from Koszyce survived and witnessed the liberation.[76]

---

76 Translated from the website commemorating the Polish Jews
   http://moreshet.pl/en/node/1163

Warsaw Ghetto

In 1939, German Occupation authorities began to concentrate Poland's population of over three million Jews into a number of extremely crowded ghettos, located in the main Polish cities. The largest of these, the Warsaw Ghetto, was established by the German Governor-General on October 16, 1940, and it concentrated approximately 300,000–400,000 people into a densely packed, 3.3 km central area of Warsaw. All of the Jews in Warsaw and its suburbs were rounded up and herded into the Ghetto. At this time, the Ghetto's population was estimated to be about 30% of Warsaw's population; however, the area of the Ghetto was only about 2.4% of Warsaw. The Germans closed the Warsaw Ghetto to the outside world on November 15, 1940, by building a wall that was 3 m (9.8 ft) high and topped with barbed wire. Escapees could be shot on sight.

Thousands of Jews died, due to rampant disease and starvation, even before the mass deportations from the Ghetto to the Treblinka extermination camp began. On July 22, 1942, the Germans began an *aktion*, a massive deportation, from the Warsaw Ghetto. The deportation lasted until September 21st, and during this time, about 260,000 people were sent to the Treblinka concentration camp.

Out of the remaining occupants, many of the young people dedicated themselves to establishing an underground, whose members came from most political parties and youth movements.

When the deportations first began, members of the Jewish resistance movement met and decided not to fight the SS directives, believing that the Jews were being sent to labour camps and not to their deaths. By the end of 1942, however, Ghetto inhabitants had learned that the deportations were part of an extermination process. Many of the remaining Jews decided to revolt. The first armed resistance in the ghetto occurred in January 1943.

On January 18, 1943, the Germans began another *aktion*. The leadership of the Jewish underground assessed that this was planned to be the final deportation from the Ghetto, and reacted with force and in what was named "The Small Uprising." While Jewish families hid in their so-called "bunkers," Jewish underground fighters resisted, engaging the Germans in direct clashes. Though the Jewish fighters suffered heavy losses (including some of their leaders), the Germans also suffered casualties, and the deportation was halted within a few days. Only 5,000 Jews were removed, instead of the 8,000 planned. After the demonstration of resistance, the Germans stopped the *aktion*. This presented a turning point for the Jews in the Ghetto. They believed that the *aktion* had been stopped as a result of the resistance, and therefore, many adopted the way of the underground, and began preparing hiding places in the bunkers that had been built in the cellars, and mounting a resistance.

On April 19, 1943, Passover eve, the Germans entered the Ghetto. The remaining Jews knew that the Germans would murder them, and they decided to resist to the last breath. The Nazi force that entered the Ghetto consisted of several thousand troops. After initial setbacks, the Germans systematically burned and blew up the Ghetto's buildings, block by block, rounding up or murdering anyone they could capture. Significant resistance ended on April 28, and the Nazi operation officially ended in mid-May, culminating with the demolition of the Great Synagogue of Warsaw on May 16. There were 13,000 Jews killed in the Ghetto during the uprising (some 6,000 of whom were burnt alive or died from smoke inhalation). According to the German casualty lists, German forces suffered a total of 110 casualties; 17 dead and 93 injured. Of the remaining approximately 50,000 residents, most were captured and shipped to concentration and extermination camps, in particular to Treblinka.[77]

---

77 Translated from the website of the Holocaust Resource Center, The International School for Holocaust Studies, Yad Vashem.

The Polish Uprising

The Polish uprising began on August 1, 1944, following a command given by the *Armia Krajowa* (Polish Underground Home Army). The uprising was expected to take control over Warsaw a short while prior to the expected entry of the Red Army, and to take revenge against the Nazi enemy.

The insurgents, however, were unaware that the Germans had decided to defend their 'fortress' of Warsaw and to counterattack Red Army forces situated to the east of the city. Warsaw's insurgents, an estimated 40,000 soldiers, including 4,000 women, had only enough weapons for 2,500 fighters. They were facing a 15,000-strong German garrison, which would grow to a force of 30,000, armed with tanks, planes and artillery.

Four days after the beginning of the uprising, the Germans started their offensive, which included mass executions of approximately 65,000 civilians in the captured districts. Poles, without regard for age or gender, were rounded up house by house and shot. The allied forces did not extend much help. Their assistance included only a few drops of armament. In mid-September, the Soviet air force performed a few drops of ammunition and food.

Although the vast majority of the resistance in Warsaw included members of the Home Army, there were a small number of fighters who weren't members of that organization. In the course of the uprising, some 1,700 members of other resistance organizations joined the uprising. Those included the Armia Ludowa, Gwardia Ludowa, and Narodowe Siły Zbrojne. The Armia Ludowa fighters included a group of Jews—members of the Jewish Combat Organization (Polish: Żydowska Organizacja Bojowa, ŻOB) who had succeeded to escape from the Warsaw Ghetto Uprising after the repression.

On August 4, the rebels liberated a few hundred Greek and Hungarian Jews who had been interned in the concentration camp on Gesia Street, and they joined the fighting as members of aid units. The civil population of Warsaw supported the uprising by publishing manifestos, organizing first aid, supplies, mail services and so on.

On September 5, after the Germans demolished the Old City and the Wola neighborhood, they also occupied Powisle. Two weeks later, the Germans held the entire left bank of the Wisla River. Polish troops that had been parachuted in earlier took hold of the right bank of the river and succeeded, in spite of numerous losses, to mobilize a few regiments to reach the left bank. They could not, however, succeed in aiding the rebels.

On September 27, the Mokotów quarter surrendered, and on September 30, the Żoliborz surrendered. The isolated center of the city surrendered on October 2, 1944, and this marked the end of the uprising. The Polish losses reached 16,000-20,000 dead and missing fighters, 7,000 wounded and approximately 150,000 civilians killed. This number included a few thousand Jews who had been hiding amongst the Polish population after the annihilation of the ghetto.

The Germans deported most of the civilian population to the Proszkow, Piastow and Orzerow camps. From there, around 65,000 were taken to concentration camps, around 100,000 were sent to forced labor camps in the Reich, and the rest were scattered in the territory of the *Generalgouvernement*.[78] Even after the surrender

---

78 General Government—a German zone of occupation established by Adolf Hitler after the joint invasion of Poland by Nazi Germany and the Soviet Union in 1939, at the onset of World War II. The newly-occupied Second Polish Republic was split into three zones: the General Government in its center, Polish areas annexed by Nazi Germany in the west and Polish areas annexed by the Soviet Union in the east.

of the rebels, the Germans continued to demolish and burn down the untouched parts of the city. As a result of the uprising and the total destruction of the city, Polish cultural treasures were severely damaged.[79]

The Magenta Immigrants' Camp, Italy

In 1945, a transit camp for immigrants opened in Villa Fasano near Magenta and operated under the disguise of a school for agriculture. The castle belonged to an Italian count who wanted to atone for his collaboration with the fascists and became a protector of the Jews.

During a short period of becoming organized, the castle was renovated by units that had arrived from Israel. Large quantities of supplies were stolen from the storages of the British army (beds, mattresses, blankets, gas barrels, kitchen equipment, etc.) and brought over to the camp. Underground storage places were dug, and the equipment for the immigration ships as well as ammunition were hidden there.

Within a short period of time, hundreds of young people who were waiting for their immigration arrived at the camp. Coaches from the various youth movements that were active in Israel at that time (HaShomer HaTzair, HaMahanot HaOlim, Dror, etc.) came to guide them. The young people who stayed in the camp had different tasks, which included the preparation of food and medicine boxes for the ships, sewing hammocks that were used as beds on the ships and sewing backpacks for the immigrants' personal affects. Cultural activities were organized in the evenings.

---

79 Translated from the website of the Holocaust Resource Center, The International School for Holocaust Studies, Yad Vashem.

The Immigrants' Ship Shabtai Luzinski

The ship was named after Shabtai Luzinski, who arrived in Italy after the war and contributed much in organizing the immigrants. The team in charge of preparing the ship included Avraham Zakai, Avraham Shavut, Bezalel Drori, others from *Eretz Yisrael* and local Italians. A construction made of iron pipes that included 600 beds was put together inside the ship. Eight toilets were installed, food was brought from storages near Milan, as well as water and gas; all were financed by the Joint. The ship was equipped with five rubber boats and a wooden boat for the 15 accompanying Palyam team members: David Maimon (Snapir), who was the ship's commander; Bezalel Freiman Drori (Yashka), who was in charge of the organization and wellbeing of the immigrants; Ossi Ravid, Avraham Karni-Rickman (Gesher) and three of the Haganah members in Europe: Yonna, Shlomo and Sasha. The *gidoni* (communication person) was Arieh Haikind. The captain was Italian, but in actuality, David Maimon occupied this position.

The ship sailed from Metaponto Harbor in South Italy on March 4, 1947. At the same time, and in order to ease the crowdedness of the first few days, another 173 immigrants sailed with the ship Albertina. Five days later, the passengers of Albertina were moved to Shabtai Luzinski, and then, all together, the ship carried 823 passengers. Amongst the passengers were 130 men who had been trained in Europe by the Haganah, as part of the organization's plan for Aliya Gimmel—an armed and forceful landing on the shores of Israel, which was eventually canceled. The trip organizers were careful to camouflage the ship, and therefore the immigrants stayed most of the time in the ship's belly.

The route of the ship was along the shores of Italy, through Santa Maria, Cape Matapan, the Stampalia Island and Cape Gelidonya in the southern coast of Turkey, on to the Libyan coasts, along the Egyptian shore and ultimately to Nitzanim Beach.

On the morning of departure, at 9 am, an unidentified airplane circled the ship from above and flew away. During the days of the travel by sea, no contact was made with the British planes or destroyers. The immigrants were given standard orders regarding passive resistance in the case of capture. No confrontation took place on the sea; the ship was discovered only when it reached the shore. The escorts were ordered to mingle with the immigrants and to sneak away.

The drop off was on Nizanim beach, where, due to the small number of Jewish settlements, British security was lower. The ship approached the beach on March 12 without being discovered, but due to the stormy sea, the immigrants could not be lowered into the rubber boats from fear that they would capsize. It was decided to beach the ship on the shore. The ship was heading towards the beach when it hit a sand shoal 120 meters away from it. In the meantime, daylight broke, and out of concern from being discovered, it was decided to stretch a rope from the shore to the ship and transport along it the boats with the immigrants. Those who could swim jumped off the ship and started swimming towards the shore, while the Haganah members who waited on shore and the Playam members who were accompanying the ship, directed their journey in the water. Afterwards, some of the immigrants who had arrived on shore managed to scatter and hide in the neighboring settlements. Three hours after the beginning of the disembarking, British soldiers from the nearby camp surrounded the area, while the project of disembarking and organizing the beach was at its peak.

Hundreds of Jews from the nearby settlements were called into action, in order to prevent the deportation of the immigrants. They mingled with the immigrants and burnt their identity cards, and anyone who was asked for their identity replied: "I am a Jew from *Eretz Yisrael*." The British found it difficult to identify the immigrants and detained 900 out of the people who were on the beach.

The newspaper *Davar* reported about British soldiers as well as British and Arab policemen looting the belongings of the captured immigrants. The detainees were taken to Haifa on a journey that lasted 11 hours, and at noontime of March 13, 1947, they were taken on board the deportation ship Empire Rival, which transported them to the deportation camps in Cyprus, while about 240 of them who had been identified as Israelis remained in *Eretz Yisrael*. An additional group of 138 detainees was deported at midnight of March 15, 1947, in the Empire Shelter ship (Dina and Bezalel were part of this second group).

In March 1947, the British returned 301 of the deportees from Cyprus, and on March 28, 1947, they returned 75 more, who had been identified as residents of *Eretz Yisrael*[80] (Dina and Bezalel were amongst them).

---

80 Translated from the documentation of the Israel Navy Veterans association (I.N.V.A.)

The Submarine INS Dakar

The INS Dakar was the former modified British T-class submarine Totem of the Royal Navy that was initially put into service towards the end of World War II. In 1965, it was purchased by Israel as part of a group of three T-class submarines. The submarine underwent renovation in the Portsmouth shipyard, and, manned with an Israeli crew that had been trained by the British Navy and departed for Israel on 9 January 1968, it disappeared on January 25, en route with all of its 69 sailors.

At 06:10 on January 25, the Dakar transmitted her position, 34.16°N 26.26°E, just east of Crete. Over the next 18 hours, she sent three control transmissions, which did not include her position, the last at 00:02 January 25, 1968. No further communications were received. In spite of the broad international search carried out by ships, submarines and airplanes, and a rescue operation that included units from Israel, Great Britain, the United States, Greece, Turkey and Lebanon, the Dakar was not discovered and was declared missing. The information and the estimations regarding the cause of the submarine's disappearance were never published, and the Israeli public was faced with a mystery and a national tragedy.

On February 9, 1969, over a year after the Dakar went missing, a fisherman found her stern emergency buoy marker washed up on the coast of Khan Yunis, a town southwest of Gaza. Mistaken conclusions drawn out of the analysis of the buoy and the location where it had been found resulted in futile searches along the Egyptian shores and the Aegean Sea.

It was not until April 1999, and some 25 failed expeditions later, that a search effort was concentrated along the path of the original route. On May 24, 1999, a joint U.S.–Israeli search team using information received from U.S. intelligence sources and led by subcontractor Thomas Kent Dettweiler of the American Nauticos Corporation, detected a large body on the seabed between Crete and Cyprus, at a depth of some 3,000 meters. On May 28, the first video pictures were taken, making it clear that the Dakar had been found. She rests on her keel, bow to the northwest, approximately 485 kilometers away from her destination.

The reasons for the Dakar's sinking remain unknown to this very day.[81]

81 Translated from the website of the Clandestine Immigration and Naval Museum.

Made in the USA
Lexington, KY
13 June 2018